Education Strategy in a Changing Society

Placing the UK in a global context, this book engages with the emerging international debate on the future of education in the 21st century. It examines the post-pandemic paradigm shift in educational practice in countries around the world and presents international case studies of emerging future practice.

However, while it embraces the global context and the mega-forces therein, it is specifically focused on the challenges for education in England today and the potential strategies for moving forward to the all-inclusive, personalised, smarter and lifelong learning needed for tomorrow. In doing so, it explores how the new curriculum models, new approaches to pedagogy and new educational technology, such as AI and even robotics, might help to transform education in England, help "level-up" learning and help younger generations cope not only with the future as we know it but also the future that we don't.

This book will appeal to policymakers, students and scholars interested in the sociology of education, education policy, international education, international development and future studies, as well as those with a general interest in Education in the future.

Martin Slattery is a retired Sixth-Form College Principal and Senior Education Officer who has previously written a number of introductory and specialist texts in Sociology including *The ABC of Sociology* (1985), *Urban Sociology* (1985), *Official Statistics* (1986) and *Key Ideas in Sociology* (2003). Since retiring, he has focused on the emerging topic of Ageing and Longevity in the 21st century with the publication of *The Ageing of Great Britain* in 2019 and *The New Sociology of Ageing* in 2022.

Routledge Advances in Sociology

For more information about this series, please visit: https://www.routledge.com/Routledge-Advances-in-Sociology/book-series/SE0511

Education Strategy in a Changing Society

Personalised, Smarter,
Lifelong Learning in
the 21st Century

Martin Slattery

R Routledge
Taylor & Francis Group

LONDON AND NEW YORK

First published 2024
by Routledge
4 Park Square, Milton Park, Abingdon, Oxon OX14 4RN

and by Routledge
605 Third Avenue, New York, NY 10158

Routledge is an imprint of the Taylor & Francis Group, an informa business

© 2024 Martin Slattery

British Library Cataloguing-in-Publication Data
A catalogue record for this book is available from the British Library

Library of Congress Cataloging-in-Publication Data
Names: Slattery, Martin, author.
Title: Education strategy in a changing society : personalised,
smarter, lifelong learning in the 21st century / Martin Slattery.
Description: New York : Routledge, 2024. | Series: Routledge
advances in sociology | Includes bibliographical references and
index.
Identifiers: LCCN 2023056705 (print) | LCCN 2023056706 (ebook)
| ISBN 9781032415772 (hbk) | ISBN 9781032415796 (pbk) | ISBN
9781003358770 (ebk)
Subjects: LCSH: Educational change--Case studies. | Educational
leadership--Case studies. | Continuing education--Effect of
technological innovations on. | Adult education--Curricula--
Computer-assisted instruction. | Distance education--Computer
network resources--Social aspects. | Open learning--Social aspects.
Classification: LCC LA134 .S53 2024 (print) | LCC LA134 (ebook)
| DDC 370--dc23/eng/20240122
LC record available at https://lccn.loc.gov/2023056705
LC ebook record available at https://lccn.loc.gov/2023056706

ISBN: 978-1-032-41577-2 (hbk)
ISBN: 978-1-032-41579-6 (pbk)
ISBN: 978-1-003-35877-0 (ebk)

DOI: 10.4324/9781003358770

Typeset in Times New Roman
by MPS Limited, Dehradun

This book is dedicated to the many outstanding staff and inspiring students that I have worked with over the past 40 years in 4 counties across the UK. It has been a pleasure and a privilege; a personal and professional journey of a lifetime. Thank You All So Much.

And my undying thanks as always to my wife Jacqueline for her love, patience and support throughout this project; and to our children and nine wonderful grandchildren as they embark on their lifelong journey into a century like no other. I hope that they realise all their dreams and enjoy great happiness on the way.

Finally, my thanks, as always, to Emily Briggs, my editor in having faith in this project, to Manmohan Negi, my project manager for his professionalism in producing it, and to Lakshita Joshi, my editorial assistant, for her support throughout.

Contents

Introduction

"The illiterate of the 21st century will not be those who cannot read and write, but those who cannot learn, unlearn, and relearn." Alvin Toffler & Herbert Gerjuoy (1970)

Education systems across the world are in turmoil not only because they are trying to "catch-up" after the Covid-19 lockdown but because many question whether the models of education developed in the late 20th century are still "fit for purpose" in the 21st century. "A generation ago, teachers could expect that what they taught would last their students a lifetime. Today, because of rapid economic and social change, schools have to prepare students for jobs that have not yet been created, technologies that have not yet been invented and problems that we don't yet know will arise". Andreas Schleicher (OECD Director of Learning: 2018).

With education in England once again a "hot topic" following the Prime Minister's endorsement of the idea that a British Baccalaureate might provide a suitable framework for future post-16 education in England, *Education, Education, Education* may once again be back on the political and election agenda. Certainly, the present system of education in England has been subject to increasing criticism in recent years; criticisms that it is failing to meet the educational needs of a post-Brexit Britain entering the Fourth Industrial Revolution; failing to provide the breadth of curriculum and develop the 21st-century life skills needed by young people today entering the digital world of work tomorrow; failing to provide the equality of opportunity needed for all pupils to progress according to their potential. And worse perpetuating, if not legitimising, inequalities in both opportunity and outcome. Critics see the English education system as essentially an industrial model of mass education based on an outdated, narrow and academic-dominated curriculum overshadowed by an oppressive examination and assessment system; one that David Priestland of the Guardian described in January 2013 as "the most tested in the industrialised world" with league tables

DOI: 10.4324/9781003358770-1

that "force teachers to 'teach to the test', demoralising the profession and demotivating students". Professor Stephen Ball (2018) has gone further and questioned whether England has an education system at all "Rather than having an educational system in England, we have a rickety, divided and often unstable, but nonetheless, overbearing, educational apparatus. tenuously held together by a regime of testing and league tables". Such has been the level of criticism that in 2021, the editor of the Times, John Witherow, concluded that "it's time to take stock and see what needs to be done to reform it to give young people a better start in life"; a decision that led to the setting up of the Times Education Commission (TEC); a Commission that produced a withering report in 2022. The House of Lords Select Committee in December 2023 went even further declaring that secondary education in England "Requires Improvement" and "urgent change" including the abandonment of the E'Bacc, one of the pillars of the current government's policy on 11–16 curriculum and assessment so setting the case and helping to inform the momentum for radical change in English education in a year that is likely to see a British General Election.

These failings and this mismatch of education to the needs of society in the 21st century, however, is not just a British concern. Rather, it is an international fear. The WEF declared in January 2022 that the world is facing a Global Educational Crisis "a learning crisis (with) more than 250 million primary and secondary school aged children and youth are out of school; one third have never been to school"; a "crisis within a crisis" as Covid-19 closed schools across the world and brutally exposed the underlying weaknesses of national systems of education; education systems that the WEF described in 2021 as "relics of the past". "We may be living through the Fourth Industrial Revolution, yet our schools and education systems still resemble those from the First" (October 2021) The world of the 21st century is changing fast and fundamentally. Megaforces such as globalisation, social media and mass urbanisation are reshaping our social landscape; Smart-technology, artificial intelligence (AI) and the superhighway are reshaping the world economy; the Asian Tigers of the East are intensifying their challenge against the Amazons, Apples, Googles and Facebooks of the West while China, Russia and the emerging nations of India and East Asia are threatening to undermine if not overturn the post-war economic order created some 75 years ago. Meanwhile, beneath such titanic political and economic struggles, the human race is ageing fast, global migration is accelerating at speed and the whole planet seems to be in an existential crisis in the face of climate change, global pandemics, AI, cyberwarfare, social media and the rise of authoritarian states threatening to disrupt and overturn the post-war global political order with Russia's invasion of Ukraine and Hamas's attack on Israel, just the latest examples. In the face of such a fast-changing, turbulent and unpredictable world, high-quality education is essential. Yet the education systems designed for the relatively stable worlds of the late 20th century struggle to prepare young people today for the challenges and lifestyles of tomorrow. They need, in many commentators' view, a fundamental rethink; a radical redesign and a new underlying paradigm. They need a new set of aims and ambitions if they are to serve the needs and the aspirations of society, employers and parents for the future; if they are to develop the full potential of each and every student and prepare them for a future that is increasingly unpredictable, highly disruptive and politically, economically and socially explosive. Covid-19 has ruthlessly exposed and amplified many of these challenges and inequalities but it has equally opened up the potential for radical change and for accelerating the shift to new technology and new ways of learning in the 100-year life ahead. Remote learning, personalised tutoring, libraries of e-learning materials for all ages and new types of educational examination and assessment are all initiatives that were barely thinkable prior to lockdown some four years ago and yet which are now fuelling a more fundamental debate and re-examination of the purpose and design of education in the 21st century. As Sir Anthony Seldon has forcefully argued (2018) "our politicians, educators and administrators the world over are asleep to the 4th education revolution hurtling towards us. We are failing our young people, our countries and the world by not adapting quickly enough to how AI will change the way that education takes place, the jobs it is preparing them for, and the society in which we will live".

The 21st century increasingly needs a new vision and a new ambition for learning; for Personalised, Smarter, Life-Long Learning for the 100-year life ahead if it is to maximise the power and potential—economic, political and personal—not only of future generations but also for its older ones too. As Andreas Schleicher of the OECD (2018) has argued, students in the 21st century "will need to develop curiosity, imagination, resilience, and self-regulation; they will need to respect and appreciate the ideas, perspectives and values of others; they will need to cope with failure and rejection, and move forward in the face of adversity. Their motivation will be more than getting a good job and a high income; they will also need to care about the well-being of their friends and family, their communities and the planet". There is mounting need, according to Sean Tierney, Director of Learning at Microsoft (2020), for a new educational Vision and Mission; a new culture and ethos of learning: a shift from "a teaching culture to a learning culture", one designed to empower students to learn for themselves in flexible, often collaborative ways, inside and outside classrooms, at their own pace; while teachers will need to have access to real-time data on how each student is progressing scholastically and emotionally; and parents will need to be better connected to, and involved in, their children's education with certainty, detail and confidence.

So, education in the 21st century has become something of a global mission; an international search for a new holy grail with international organisations such as the OECD, WEF, World Bank and UNESCO leading the way and putting enormous resources into defining and designing schemes for education in the 21st century. Schemes ranging from the OECD's Compass for Learning, the WEF's Education 4.0 and UNESCO's New Social Contract for Education, each with its own version of the essential learning skills needed for living and working in the years ahead; each with its own ideas on the curriculum for the future; each with its own strategy on smart learning and the potential impact of new technology on personalising learning and liberating teaching. They all point, however, to the need for a new set of educational strategic aims and objectives; to a shift from *school performance to pupil progression;* from educating the young to providing life-long learning for all ages; from sifting out the academically able, to developing the potential, personal skills and attributes of each and every learner whatever their age. Such fundamental changes in strategy and structure, however, will require more than tinkering or even reform of the existing educational system. They will require a fundamental change; a paradigm shift in:

• Structure and strategy; a shift from mass education age 5–24, monopolised by such educational institutions as schools and colleges to personalised learning for life, age 3–100.
• Curriculum and content from the narrow, academic knowledge-based curriculum of today to broader skills-based curriculum of tomorrow; from age-related terminal testing at 16, 18 and 21 to life-long personalised profiling and skill development;
• Teaching and learning; from teacher-led learning to a learning partnership, from the *Sage on Stage* to teachers operating more as coaches and learning managers with students acting as peer mentors, innovators and team leaders, from learning alone to learning as part of a team; a team that might include avatars, AI and robotic playmates as well as specialist tutors particularly for students with special needs, disabilities or from disadvantaged backgrounds.
• Assessment and qualifications; from bolt-on systems of external exam-inations and qualifications attained during the early years of formal education (5–24) to a personal and professional portfolio of skill development and accreditation throughout life in the century ahead.

Achieving this shift, redesigning the strategic aims, ambitions and architecture of education across any country will be an educational and political challenge of immense proportions that will test the political skill of even the most seasoned of politicians and the political commitment and endurance of government irrespective of who is in power. Instituting such fundamental change in a country as diverse as the UK will involve even greater complexity. While Scotland and Wales have sought to undertake a system transformation into 21st-century skills. English education seems to have gone "backwards", back to reasserting the academic tradition of the past through the grip of an English-Baccalaureate or E'Bacc, the retention of a terminal examination system (GCSE) at age 16 and an Ofsted inspection regime that seems to do more to "name and blame" schools rather than act as a "critical friend". Promoting performance and innovation through the current "standards" and market approach to English education seems to legitimise inequality rather than "level it up".

So, while Chapter 1 of this book seeks to explore the 21st-century challenges facing education today in the UK and the world at large, Chapter 2 attempts to identify the global forces that seem most likely to impact the learning and life skills of students born into a 21st century that is already as chaotic, unpredictable and life-changing as any century before. Chapter 3 seeks to draw out from the mushrooming international debate, the learning and life skills most needed for children and young people entering the mid-21st century, the potential impact of new educational technology and the insights and experience derived from today's leading educational nations in implementing educational change, while Chapter 4 attempts to sketch out what a new paradigm for education in England in the 21st century might begin to look like; one that not only embraces new technologies such as AI and robotics but adopts new models of assessment and administration. The resultant strategy, agenda and educational framework suggested is not, therefore, intended to be just a theoretical exercise but a practical proposal; a contribution to an educational debate that has been simmering beneath the surface across the UK even before Covid-19 lockdown; one that has helped fuel the growing dissatisfaction amongst employers and amongst teachers in recent years and now, one that has at last emerged as one of the Great Debates for the next British General Election. "Education, Education, Education" Part 2 seems at last to be back on the political agenda precisely at a time when it is gathering pace globally. As the Learning Policy Institute argued back in 2020, "Now is the time to reimagine traditional structures and practices; to rethink the way in which schools are organized around time, physical space, educator expertise, curriculum, and instruction; and redesign schools around principles of authentic learning, stronger relationships, and wraparound supports centered on the whole child". So, what might a strategy for making Education in England more "Personalised, Smarter and Life-Long in the 21st century ahead" and so better able to compete with such emerging leading lights as China, Singapore, Estonia and Scandinavia, actually look like. And what is to be learnt too from the rest of the UK—Scotland, Wales and even North Ireland—in their journeys towards a new educational landscape? What is so wrong with the English education system? Why do many commentators believe that it needs fundamental transformation not just another reform?

Bibliography

Ball Stephen: The Education Debate: 4th edition: Policy Press (2021)

Global Market Insights (2021)

House of Lords Select Committee Report: Requires Improvement: Urgent Change for 11-16 Education (December 12, 2023)

Learning Policy Institute(LPI): Reinventing School in the COVID Era and Beyond: Darling-Hammond L et al (September 2020)

Priestland David: *Britain's Education System is Being Tested to Destruction*: Opinion: Education Policy (January 13, 2013)

Schleicher Andreas: *The Future of Education and Skills*: Education 2030 (Foreword): OECD (2018)

Seldon Anthony with Abidoye Oladimeji: *The Fourth Educational Revolution*: The University of Buckingham Press (2018 & 2020)

Toffler Alvin & Gerjuoy Herbert: *Future Shock*: Turtleback Books (1970)

Tierney Sean: *Director of Learning at Microsoft*: Schools after COVID-19: (June 17, 2020)

Times Education Commission: *Bringing out the Best*: How to Transform Education and Unleash the Potential of Every Child (June 2022)

WEF: Schools Must Lead the Way in Education Reform (October 4, 2021)

WEF: The Global Education Crisis Is Even Worse than We Thought (January 16, 2022)

1   The Crisis in Education Today

"Every country on earth at the moment is reforming public education" for two reasons-economic and cultural. However, "The problem is that they're trying to meet the future by doing what they did in the past. And on the way they are alienating millions of kids who don't see any purpose in going to school"
Ken Robinson (2016)

The Background

The UK does not have a common education system. All four education systems in the UK today are devolved to the national administrations of England, Scotland, Wales and North Ireland. So, while the primary focus of this chapter is on education in England, the contrast in educational strategies is stark with England embarking on a journey back to its academic past over the last 14 years, while the rest of the UK has, with OECD support, embarked on wholesale and long-term educational reforms for the future; reforms that may well have substantive lessons for England too. Secondly, the UK itself is changing rapidly and decisively with huge implications for its future economically, politically and socially. The UK is still recovering from a financial crisis in 2008 that ushered in an era of austerity ever since, a Brexit Referendum in 2016 that still polarises public opinion, a Covid-19 global pandemic that locked down world society and now a cost-of-living crisis following Russia's invasion of Ukraine; all building up to a forthcoming British General Election and a judgement on where England and the UK go next after 14 years of primarily Conservative rule. Beneath that social and political surface lies a demographic revolution of tectonic proportions as Britain's population ages, its demography diversifies and its nations and regions fragment politically and economically as revealed in the 2021 Census.

Meanwhile, the education system in England seems to be suffering not only from crumbling concrete but also from a collapse in the whole edifice that is English education. As Professor Stephen Ball scathingly

DOI: 10.4324/9781003358770-2

described it in his Sir John Cass Foundation lecture in March 2018, "The tragedy of state education in England is that there is no system at all; rather than a unified system of state education, English education has been subjected a set of competing subsystems that jostle, grate and overlap; a post-code lottery whereby the school your child may attend and their experience of education depend on where you live"; an education system that has experienced the paradigm shifts from the post-war tripartite system of grammar, secondary modern and occasionally technical schools to the comprehensive movement heralded by Circular 10/65, the explosion of higher education after the Robbins Report of 1963; the liberalisation of primary education after the Plowden Report of 1967, the National Curriculum introduced in 1988 and the drive thereafter to create a market system of education based on competing schools (and colleges), performance testing and league tables. Successive Conservative, Labour and Coalition governments have sought to drive up educational standards, increase parental choice and replace local authority control and oversight with a mishmash of school autonomy, multi-academy trusts and centralised dictates generated by a succession of Ministers of Education, each with their own priorities, ideologies and reform agendas, many of whom were in office for less than two years let alone the time needed to see their reforms through. In Professor Ball's view, we now have such a profusion of school types and lines of accountability that it is difficult to see who is running England's education system and in what direction. It operates in such segmented silos and sectors that few at the top or bottom of England's current education system can clearly see what they have created or steer its direction of travel. England's educational landscape is littered with everything from academies and free schools through to grammar and comprehensive schools, community schools, trust schools, special schools, church and faith schools and university technical colleges. Worse, current educational policy seems to suffer from "policy hyper-activity", a pandora's box of initiatives and priorities driven by "ministerial enthusiasms and biases, international orthodoxies, and ad hoc, often ill-informed and ill-thought-out borrowings from other systems" (Morris P: 2012) Schools are expected to be "both innovative and conservative, to deliver social mobility and social cohesion..to be collaborative and entrepreneurial". They are subjected to a constant barrage of new initiatives, funding streams and new regulations alongside changing targets and performance measures. They alone are held accountable for pupil performance and behaviour despite sustained research that to-date schools have only a limited impact on attainment; as little as 9% according to Wilkinson et al (2018). By far the greater part of variance in student attainment is explained by social background, family life and parental education and support. "Education policy is looking at and working on the wrong place and is bound to fail if the socio-economic conditions of students' lives remain dramatically unequal". No-one would start from where we are with English education. What is needed, argues Ball, is a different set of organising principles and "concomitantly staged but unequivocal abandonment of the current education policy infrastructure"; "converting them from exam factories to communities of discovery", rebuilding trust in teachers and schools and by tackling the relationship between education, inequality and poverty by "the educative engagement of schools with their communities".

A dramatic and shattering overview of the English education system but, unfortunately, one supported by many historians and social scientists. According to the educational historian Derek Gillard (2018) while education was one of the great pillars of the British Welfare State created after WWII, it was, in many ways, doomed from the start and contained the seeds of its own destruction. While the 1944 Education Act: "was undoubtedly an enormous achievement-all the more remarkable for having been conceived in the depths of a horrific world war", it was fundamentally flawed from its inception; an administrative rather than an educational structure; a compromise between the diverse interests predominant in English education from national and local government through to educational lobby groups such as the churches and charities. "The curriculum and pupil learning barely got a look-in". The 1944 Education Act failed to resolve the key issues of the continued involvement of the churches in state education and in particular, it allowed a separate elitist and independent public school system to continue to survive and thrive, aided by its charitable status and separate regulatory and inspection system. Far from the 1944 Education Act abolishing social class in post war Britain as part of the New Jerusalem promised by the post-war Labour Government, it and subsequent educational reforms such as the 11 plus examination and tripartite system of secondary education, tended to strengthened and legitimised it. Labour governments thereafter never truly overcame this fundamental fault line—and politically, never really tried to do so. The Labour Government of 1964–1979 was certainly an explosion of educational opportunity with the Raising of the School Leaving Age (ROSLA), the Plowden Revolution in primary education, the explosion in Higher Education after the Robbins Report and the introduction of a National Curriculum. Such radical steps forward in opening up educational opportunity, however, were not matched by the shift from tripartite to comprehensive secondary education; a radical shift in itself but one softened by it being introduced by an advisory Circular (10/65) rather than by a statutory Education Act, allowing overt and covert selection to remain a feature of English education ever since. It equally failed to distinguish between two apparently opposing concepts of comprehensive education—the egalitarian and the meritocratic; the education for all irrespective of ability and the selection on merit judged by academic performance; two very different philosophies of education and expectations of outcome.

In contrast, to such social and educational optimism, the 1970s quickly became an era of retrenchment and recession; an era of mass unemployment and class conflict culminating in the election of Mrs Thatcher in 1979 and a wholesale attack on any notion of comprehensive education led by the Black Papers and **New Right** Government. Thatcher's second administration was aimed at "the destruction of the post-war settlement and the ways in which it organised social, economic and political life" (Jones: 2003); as Britain polarised into something of an ideological class war between the government and unions, central government and left-wing local authorities, the liberal left and the New Right. The introduction of competition and market forces into education through LMS and parental choice alongside the diminishing of local authority controls and devolution of power to school governors were part of this dismantling of the Education State alongside severe cuts in the state education budget from 6.5% of GDP in 1975–1976 to 4.7% by 1988/1989. State schools were described as hotbeds of left-wing radicalism; Keith Joseph as Education Secretary led the Conservative drive on school standards while Norman Tebbit led the attack on the permissive society, defining the fight for education as a fight for the moral health of the nation amid intense public debates about sex education and gay rights. The 1988 Education Act, LMS, GM School status, CTCs and the abolition of the ILEA were all shifts away from local education controls to an English education system under direct rule from the Department of Education on the one hand and from market forces under school governors on the other hand. The new 16 plus GCSE examining system was introduced in 1987 and regulated not by the examining boards but by central government so giving the Minister of Education control not only over the National Curriculum but over its examination.

The election of **New Labour** after nearly 20 years of political turbulence and economic crisis appeared to represent a return to consensus and comprehensive ideals. However, the New Labour Mantra *Education, Education, Education* was in the view of many educational historians a continuation of Conservative policies on parental choice, market forces and performance management as much as an attempt to mitigate social and educational inequality. School diversity increased with the advent of Faith Schools, specialist colleges and City academies. School and College management became more business-like, commercial sponsorship and privatisation in various forms were used to create Education Action Zones, to tackle failing LEAs such as Hackney, Liverpool and Leicester, to regenerate failing schools through the new academies programme and to fund the massive "Building Schools (and Colleges) for the Future" (BSF) programme of £45 billion through PFI (private finance initiative). There was an equally strong investment in social and educational policy in seeking to improve children and young peoples' start in life and their long-term opportunities; programmes such as the Sure Start programme, the creation of individual learning accounts and the University for Industry alongside curriculum reforms such as the new 14–19 Diplomas to integrate academic and vocational pathways post-16, to engage schools and colleges in educational partnerships, and to link-up them up with local businesses. However, New Labour's Third Way emphasised meritocracy rather than equality, diversity rather than equal opportunity and England's long tail of under-achievement pre and post-16 stubbornly remained.

In stark contrast to this era of educational investment, the **Coalition Government of 2010–2015** with Michael Gove as Education Secretary (2010–2012) was an era of economic austerity with school budgets slashed, BSF cancelled, university fees raised and the 14–19 Diploma programme abandoned following the financial collapse of 2008. It was also an era of school academisation across the sector, not just for *failing schools* but for all schools alongside a drive on educational standards with the introduction of the English Baccalaureate or E'Bacc to strengthen academic rigour in the curriculum alongside the abandonment of teacher-assessed coursework in exams and the tougher Ofsted regime reforms led by Michael Wilshaw. Michael Gove wanted to restore traditional standards and a more rigorous and academic system of education driven by a combination of tough national standards and competitive school market. He regarded the Education Establishment as a "Blob" resistant to change but ultimately his neo-liberal snow-storm of initiatives failed to take root, gain teachers or parents trust or raise the overall performance of the English education system. Rather it fragmented, disrupted and alienated much of the education sector with disadvantaged pupils, already facing the worst of the Coalitions austerity cutbacks, often the worst affected. The **Conservative Administrations** since 2015 have either been buried beneath the Brexit Debate under Theresa May or overwhelmed by Covid-19, accusations of corruption and the Partygate scandal that became features of the Johnson regime and eventually led to his resignation in July 2022. The Truss administration lasted a mere five weeks after its disastrous mini-budget in October 2022 followed by the administration of Rishi Sunak through to today; a period of political transition and turbulence that saw the passage of four PMs, four Chancellors, and five Education Secretaries in less than a year (2021/2022). The only education policy paper of note during this period was the 2022 Opportunity for All White Paper which sought to accelerate the school academisation programme to a fully trust-led system by 2030, introduce innovative and high-quality 16–19 Free Schools as well as embark on a post- Covid-19 catch-up programme and "levelling up" disadvantaged areas through Education Investment Areas; an overall strategy that *The Times* (March 28, 2022) described as "disappointingly light on ambition and substance" given the huge loss in learning during lockdown, the vast reservoir of underachievement with a third of pupils failing to pass GCSE Maths & English and the huge skills gap identified by employers in school leavers today. "A curriculum of the past not the future "and "one that blatantly failed to deal with the core issue of teacher pay, recruitment, morale and engagement"; issues that exploded in a wave of strikes in 2023.

As the educational historian, Derek Gillard (2018) has concluded, the post-war chronology of English education has been "a sad story" of a long struggle to create for England's children an education system that values them all but which so far has done little to overcome the class divisions evident and entrenched in the late 19th century; divisions that seem to have survived even into the present century and embedded in the educational post-code lottery that today is predominantly populated by multi-academy trusts or MATs that now run most state schools; trusts that according to the Ofsted 2022 Annual Report currently have no public accountability, are outside the inspection remit of Ofsted and are no longer required to conform to the national curriculum; a lack of accountability that may well explain the scandals that beset a number of early academies and that led to financial mismanagement in excess of £745 million according to the 2018 National Audit Office (NAO) Report. Worse, as the Sutton Trust Report: Chain Effect (2018) highlighted while a small group of some twelve MATs out of the 58 sponsored MATs reviewed had indeed consistently outperformed the national average for disadvantaged pupils, the rest were at best making no difference and at worse "harming the prospects" of the very pupils that they were set up to help. As this report concluded, the policy-makers "naively disregarded" the origin of many academies in serving disadvantaged areas and their blinkered focus on external school structures rather than on the quality of teachers and learning therein has undermined them ever since. Although the Government is now aiming for all schools to be academies and members of MATs by 2030, the market model remains essentially the same albeit with a distinct trend towards much larger MATs organised more on a regional and community basis; a basis that sounds increasingly like the LEAs of the past.

Like the NHS, education has been subject to a hotbed of post-war reforms, many of which have been ill-thought through by Ministers of Education mainly from a public school backgrounds and in office for less than two years on average; 17 education secretaries in 33 years according to Michael Barber' research for the Foundation for Education Development in 2021. Like the NHS, educational reforms have swung between radical centralisers to liberal decentralisers in a never-ending and, so far, fruitless search to combine empowerment and accountability and drive up performance and outcomes. As Stephen Ball (2021) has argued since James Callaghan's Great Education Debate in 1976 there has been a fundamental shift from the principles of public service to the market forces of neo-liberal education. LEAs have been dismantled, schools and colleges performance-managed and teachers reduced to feeling cogs in an educational wheel rather than professionals in control; "teaching to the test" and processing children in sets and streams rather than as individuals still in their formative years. England's education system today continues to reflect the fears and inequalities of its 19th-century origins with ever-increasing new fixes in attempt to find solutions to previous policy failures, with schools facing an ever-growing stream of directives and regulations that all contribute to an ever-increasing and often contradictory workload. Policy in this environment is what Clarke (2012) called "fantasmatic" as educational institutions are forced to address the paradox of trying to remedy social inequalities at the institutional level within a society where inequality at large is either ignored or applauded at the national and global level.

The Critiques

Against this background, it is not surprising that the English education system has generated an ever-increasing list of fundamental criticisms that include:

Its Performance

Internationally, according to the OECD PISA League Table (2018), the UK was ranked as a mid-table performer at 14th in reading, 14th in science and 18th in mathematics. The 2022 results were similar in reading and science and improved in mathematics but still well behind China, Singapore, Scandinavia and even Estonia, a country with a population of just 1.3 million even though as the DfE PISA Report (2023) admitted the final sample of English pupils "had a somewhat higher academic attainment on average than the general population." As Andreas Schleicher, the Director of Education & Skills at the OECD, commented in 2021, the UK is "an average performer" academically and internationally; a country operating "quite a traditional school system" which seems to be driving inequality by encouraging schools to write off some children through a testing system that seems to reward *average* performance rather than nurture the talent of every child; a stark contrast to countries such as Japan where "nobody looks at your average. They look at, are all of your students succeeding?" As the Children's Commissioner identified in her 2019 Briefing, some 100,000 children leave English schools each year with nothing, having failed to achieve five acceptable GCSE grades after 11 years of formal education and £100,000 of public money with disadvantaged children and those with Special Educational Needs (SEN) likely to suffer the most. Moreover, according to the Altogether Now Report (April 2022), permanent exclusions are reaching epidemic proportions pushing young people into the hands of criminal gangs and on into prison exacerbated by "off-rolling", managed moves, home education and poor quality "alternative provision", disproportionately hitting black and ethnic male youths especially those with SEN. "The Covid-19 pandemic exacerbated already entrenched inequalities for many of the most disadvantaged students" creating a generation of young people "lost to learning".

Its Curriculum

As many critics have argued, the English education system is not just flawed. It's going in exactly the wrong direction at the wrong time in prioritising academic intelligence over all other forms of learning. According to Howard Gardner (2006), academic intelligence is but one form of intelligence and not necessarily the most important. Rather, as Ken Robinson (2016) has so passionately argued, the one skill that is essential to life in the century ahead is creativity and that has been slowly squeezed out of learning in most English secondary schools today. Instead, conformity is literally the order of the day "Schools are still pretty much organised on factory lines (with) ringing bells, separate facilities, specialised into separate subjects. We still educate children by batches; we put them through the system by age group (as though) that is the date of their manufacture" Instead of learning blossoming with age, secondary-age students soon learn that "there's (only) one answer". Divergent thinking is discouraged while collaboration, essential in real life and work, in education is punished and called cheating. Children are born creative and have an extraordinary capacity for innovation but "by the time they get to be adults, most kids have lost that capacity. They have become frightened of being wrong" Traditional school curricula are largely based on the notion that theory outweighs practice and that IQ is the ultimate measure of intelligence. On that basis, it tends to divide pupils into two groups—the academically intelligent and the practical and creative, systemically preparing the former for higher education and upper occupations while relegating the latter to the lower orders socially and occupationally. This division of labour and status is even reflected in the hierarchy of school subjects with the "harder" subjects such as maths and science elevated above the "softer" more creative, social and practical subjects such as art, social science and technology so perpetuating the myth that knowledge exists only in subject silos and that intelligence is siloed in segregated disciplines rather than recognising that in practice knowledge is manifold and interdisciplinary; that people are not either academic or creative and practical but that they are multitalented and increasingly need to be to survive and thrive. As Andreas Scheicher of the OECD explained in presenting The Case for the 21st century learning in 2010 "If we spend our whole lives in the silo of a single discipline, we cannot develop the imaginative skills to connect the dots or to anticipate where the next invention, and probable source of economic value will come from. Yet, most countries, with the possible exception of the Nordic countries, provide few incentives for students to learn and teachers to teach across disciplines".

Its Assessment

The English examination system, according to many commentators, is at the heart of the current crisis in English education. It is the "tail wagging the dog". No other country in Europe has a terminal examination system at 16 plus. No other OECD country has an examination system designed to fail a third of its young people and divide them into "sheep & goats" at such a young age. As the IAC interim report on The Future of Assessment and Qualifications in England (2021) concluded "The current (examination) system is not fit for the future; is not sufficiently reliable, authentic or fair; does not support high standards of education for all and undermines student and teacher mental health". The strain of the current examination system "does little to encourage them to become the lifelong learners needed by current and future society and the economy in England". It is inequitable and not able to provide the young people of England with the skills and competences they need to thrive in a global, 21st century environment. "There can be no more powerful case for change". George Monbiot (2022) put it even more powerfully "England's punitive exam system is only good at one thing: preserving privilege". All that exams measure is "aptitude in exams" yet they determine "the entire future course of a student's life" with some branded failures never to recover. "It's not the child who fails the system. It's the system … that fails the child". As the Leading Learner (2020) explained, the fundamental fault is that "GCSEs are currently trying to serve too many masters: acting as gateways to L3 post-16 programmes; acting as proxies for school performance and account-ability; providing pre-A-level evidence of suitability for entry to HE and finally certifying pupil's academic performance". The GCSE grading system is essentially norm-referenced; ranking and fine grading pupils under the intense pressure of two weeks of artificial and written examination season rather than measuring their academic capability against a set and consistent standard. Otherwise, in theory at least, all, or most, pupils would pass rather than a third annually fail. The GCSE examine system is an academic selection system that by its nature reflects socio-economic advantage/disadvantage as much as pupils academic performance; regional inequalities rather than national standards with the wealthier SE and London now consistently outperforming pupils elsewhere as reconfirmed in the 2023 GCSE exams when London had 28.4% of entries achieving grade 7 or above compared to only 17.6% doing so in the NE of England; a gap that according to the 2023 EPI report is widening. In Paul Johnson's view (2023) "Children still face a system that narrowly rewards particular academic skills, sets them up for failure and then puts barriers in their way, rather than showing them the best routes into rewarding work". "Just one mark" at GCSE grade C can make the difference between academic success and failure and a student's future thereafter as five good GCSE grade C and above tends to be the entry point to further and higher education and the likely career choices on offer thereafter and for future life.

Its Accountability

In England, accountability is largely driven by the national inspection regime under Ofsted, with its reports and its final grading of schools, colleges or other providers as outstanding, good, requires improvement or inadequate having a profound and enduring impact on individual schools reputation, recruitment and future. Ofsted inspections are feared if not dreaded by many teachers, headteachers and governing bodies even though in surveys, 84% of headteachers said that their inspection outcomes were fair and that parents generally respected and trusted Ofsted reports. Moreover, while there is evidence that Ofsted inspections help schools improve and provide some assurance to politicians and parents about standards and quality, this is more about schools conforming to a proscribed national curriculum and performance in its examination system rather than encouraging innovation and creativity in its teaching and learning. As the NFER study of inspection regimes in six countries, England, Australia, Japan, NZ, Singapore and Wales (2018) concluded, accountability-driven systems tend to narrow the curriculum as a result of *teaching to the test* leading to an "impoverished learning experience for lower performing pupils", to targeting borderline attainers and to *gaming the system* to exclude weaker pupils from the published results. "If Canada, Finland and Singapore do not have school inspection featured in external evaluations and these countries perform better than England in PISA tests, we must question Ofsted's future within the English system".

Progression Post-16

As Paul Johnson, Director of the IFS (2023) has commented, England does not have a well-structured, well-labelled and equally valued Progression Pathway post-16 as in many other European countries "Instead of providing opportunities and ladders up, our system too often slams doors shut ... partly because it has become increasingly focused on just one route, via university"; all else is "opaque and complex", fearsomely hard to navigate as our "education system almost seems designed to make life hard for anyone who doesn't fit the traditional academic mould". Education and Skills post-16 are restricted to an absurdly narrow curriculum, under-resourced and struggling Further Education (FE) sector, and massively overcomplicated set of vocational qualifications so continuing "to deny opportunities to millions and to inflict harm on the economy". As the Augar Report declared in 2019, FE in the UK has suffered "decades of neglect and a loss of status and prestige amongst learners, employers and the public at large".

Student and Staff Health and Wellbeing

Students and staff in the UK overall are not happy. The 2018 PISA report placed the UK 69th out of the 72 nations taking part, in terms of student satisfaction; the 2023 UNICEF Child-Wellbeing in Rich Countries (Report Card 11) ranked the UK 16th out of the 29 wealthy countries represented and the 2023 World Happiness Report put the UK 19th, sandwiched between Czechia and Lithuania with the Scandinavian countries of Finland, Denmark and Iceland in the top three and the US 15th. The 2022 Good Childhood Report found that children's happiness in the UK continues to decline especially in terms of their appearance (especially for girls), schoolwork (especially for children in low-income households) while increasing numbers of parents and carers are concerned about the impact of the pandemic and the cost-of-living crisis on their children's wellbeing. The IGPP Launch Your Career report (2021) found that 70% of secondary school pupils feel uncertain and worried about their future career prospects particularly as school career advice has declined since the first lockdown with work experience and external speaker visits less and less available. Meanwhile, the DfE report by the IFF Research & Institute of Education (2022) concluded that teachers' and leaders' working conditions are "unsustainable" due to increased workloads, particularly in terms of admin and non-teaching tasks, stress, Ofsted and declining pay resulting in crisis rates of retention and recruitment from and into teaching with nearly a third of teachers who qualified in the last ten years leaving (81,000) and with only 79% of primary and 58% of secondary school vacancies filled in 2021/2022.

Inequality and Social Mobility

The English education system seems to be riddled with inequality and immobility, partly systemic, partly historical, partly market forces and parental choice. The English "public" school system, by design and history, seems to be the most glaring example of such structural inequality given its fee-paying funding system and progression pathways that seem to be *paved with gold* unerringly transporting its graduates into top universities and top jobs. As the Sutton Trust & SMC Report on Elitist Britain (2019) concluded "Britain's Elite structures are dominated by a narrow section of the population (some 7%) drawn overwhelmingly from independent schools (39%) and Oxbridge universities (24%)notably amongst senior judges, top CS, Cabinet and top media". While there is evidence of some change towards a more comprehensive intake, the overall picture is one of "persistent inequality". Critics such as Green and Kynaston (*Guardian* January 13, 2019) go further and describe private education as an "engine of inequality" and a pathway to privilege that "not only limits the life chances of those who attend state schools but also damages society at large". Top positions in government are subsequently occupied by people who almost inevitably have "only a limited and partial understanding and empathy with the realities of everyday life as lived by most people". Yet they run the depts of government as ministers and top civil servants that impact most on peoples' lives and perpetuate the cycle of privilege that is still a feature of British society even in the 21st century. However, the English state school system itself is not exactly a haven of equal opportunity. As the EPI Education in England, Annual Report 2020 concluded "High attaining pupils in England generally perform very well by international norms- reaching world-class standards. Our biggest challenge in English education consists in the long tail of low performance which is highly correlated with poverty, special education needs, some aspects of ethnicity, and other characteristics of vulnerability". That gap "will never close without systemic change" and "there are several indications that it has begun to widen" in terms of the regional and area disparities. As the 2017 Social Mobility Commission "hotspot & coldspot" analysis illustrated while

51% of FSM (free school meal) pupils in London achieved A*–C grades in GCSE English and maths, the average across England at that time was 36% in all other regions; a result largely replicated in 2023; and that while 50% of disadvantaged pupils in Kensington and Chelsea went onto university, only 10% in Eastbourne and Barnsley did. As Paul Johnson (2023) has commented, quality does not follow need in education, rather educational disadvantage tends to reflect and reinforce socio-economic inequality with deprived areas most likely to have the lowest performing schools and the least qualified teachers in such core subjects as maths, science and modern languages. Fewer than a fifth of the poorest pupils at state schools go onto university against half of the richest and 70% of private school students showing in his view that ultimately those from better-off backgrounds "not only gain more from our education system but they earn more from it".

The 2022 Levelling-Up White Paper did, at least, recognised this damning disparity and promised a *complete system change* to break the linkage between "geography and destiny". It set out 12 national missions, a seismic shift of power from Whitehall to the regions, huge investment in infrastructure especially transport and Internet connectivity, R&D and a radical shift from departmental into interdepartmental policy-making. Nine areas were chosen to jump-start this *Devolution-Revolution* ranging from Cornwall and Derbyshire to Norfolk and Suffolk with trailblazer deals for the NE, West Midlands, Glasgow and Manchester and 55 Education Investment Areas. However, as ambitious and as transformative as such programmes might be, as critics have argued the level of funding and timescale of 2030 are both inadequate and unrealistic. Worse, the *Guardian* (Feb 2022) analysis of the Government's £4.7 billion levelling-up funding, revealed that England's wealthiest areas are receiving ten times more funding than its poorest, especially in areas with Conservative ministers, while eight councils in the most deprived areas have received nothing at that time. The 2008–2020 era of austerity and then the 2020–2021 Covid-19 crisis both exposed and exacerbated inequality in the UK and led to what the Institute of Government (2021) has called "the most disruptive period in children's education since at least the start of the Second World War" yet the DoE catch-up programme of £1.4 billion was so woefully below the £13.5 billion called for by Sir Kevan Collins that he resigned in protest. As the 2021 EPI report *Education recovery and resilience in England* illustrated, the £50 per pupil per year additional funding offered by the Department was paltry compared to the £1600 per pupil allocation in the USA and £2,500 allocation in the Netherlands leaving disadvantaged pupils in 2021 effectively "as far behind their non-disadvantaged peers as they were in 2012" (Fair Education Alliance Report:2022) However, as Bobby

Duffy and his colleagues (February 2021) discovered inequality of outcome or opportunity is not yet an issue that has either stirred or unified the country. And even within academic circles, there is an intense debate as to whether social mobility is more myth than reality. As Bukodi and Goldthorpe (2019) have ardently argued, the real engine of social mobility in Britain is not individuals moving up and down social ladders but the socio-economic structure itself shifting to a new occupational level; one that elevates whole swathes of the population upwards as happened with the vast expansion of white-collar jobs in the post-war era at the same time that traditional working-class occupations declined. As John Goldthorpe has explained unless the overall occupational structure changes dramatically, any improvement in the relative mobility chances of children of less advantaged class origins "can only come about at the expense of a worsening of the chances of children of more advantaged origins" through, for example, a breakup of glass floors and ceilings and a substantive increase in downward mobility. Any serious strategy to use education to drive or even help increase social mobility therefore needs not only a strategy and funding to support the socially disadvantaged with real investment in childcare and early learning but an equally determined strategy to offset the means by which the better-off are able to maintain their social advantage by moving school catchment area, employing private tutors or paying for private education. Schools need to receive a "balanced intake of pupils" as proposed by the Sutton Trust, politicians need to recognise that education is not a cause of social immobility or inequality but an effect and that until inequality at large is tackled, education on its own cannot make a significant or long-lasting difference. In Goldthorpe's view, the real solution is investment in lifelong adult education, the creation of a technologically driven economy and a more humane form of society in which men and women of all social origins "enjoy economic well-being, security and stability and the prospect of advancement over the course of their working lives".

Education and Employment

Employers have long been highly critical of England's education system and question whether it is any longer fit for purpose (Jason Taylor: July 2019) The 2019 Ipsos Employer's Survey, for example, concluded that "Our education system for their futures". The House of Commons Education Committee Report Dec. 2020 called for "an adult skills and lifelong learning revolution"; a shift from focusing overwhelmingly on education before the age of 25 "towards a system and culture of lifelong learning that encourages education at any age ... a comprehensive and holistic vision for lifelong learning that works for every adult in every community" engaging employers, HE and FE in a national mission to meet the lifelong skills challenges of the 21st century and so raise productivity and GDP in the UK. However, the committee concluded that "We are not persuaded that the Department fully grasps the value and purpose of community education. Nor does it appear that the Department has a vision or strategic approach for boosting this vital area of lifelong learning".

Education Spending

The 2022 IFS Annual Report on Education Spending in England 2022 identified that all forms of state education in England suffered dramatic funding cuts in the period 2010/2011 to 2019/2020 of some 8% or £10 billion in its overall budget and some 9% in school spending per pupil; "the largest cut in over 40 years". Even the proposed increase in school spending per pupil through to 2024, in their view, "will do no more than return spending to 2010 levels". Deprived schools have seen the largest cuts with the most deprived experiencing a 14% real-terms fall per pupil while spending per student 16–19 fell dramatically by 14% in colleges and 28% in school sixth-forms; falls only partially offset by the proposed rises for 2024/2025. Adult skills has suffered a similarly drastic reduction with the total adult skills spending for 2024–2025 still 22% below that in 2010–2011. Meanwhile, HE spending has steadily declined from around £11,000 per student in 2012–2013 to £9,300 in 2022–2023 with a dramatic shift of tuition and maintenance fees onto students themselves. As Paul Johnson, Director of the IFS, has commented (2023) the percentage of nation income spent on education today has changed little from the 4–5% spent in the 1980s and while the new National Funding Formula (NFF) introduced in 2018 will help make school funding more responsive, it contains "a sting in the equalisation tail" in that by promising a statutory minimum level of funding per pupil it ironically shifts funding from schools in deprived areas to those in more affluent ones.

Education Policy in England

As commentators as varied as Stephen Ball and Dominic Cummings have commented, policy-making and implementation under the British system of government is an issue of major concern in itself and one not helped by the astonishing turnover of ministers of state and the lack of consistent long-term planning. As Paul Johnson (2023) has commented, with 14 Secretaries of State in education since 2000, and "an average time in the job of less than two years, secretaries of state barely have enough time to understand the problems, let alone be part of the solution. (Instead) They can too end up being part of the problem". Like health and most other areas of policy-making, education needs stability and consistency; a long-term vision and plan derived from fact not ideological fiction, the needs of all children not just those most politically vocal or economically advantaged; an independent and an insider perspective not only of key stakeholders such as teachers and parents but of the pupils and students of the future. In Johnson's view, England remains "among the most centralised states in the developed world" presided overwhelmingly from London with local authorities a "shadow of their former selves" reduced primarily to certain local services and to overseeing social care. When Johnson joined the Dept for Education and Employment, he assumed that the role of government was to set structure, incentives and accountabilities, and let school leaders and professionals deliver within a broad framework. Instead, "I was amazed to find the department saw its role quite differently-a lot of micro-management and a focus effectively on telling teachers how to teach". The Education and Skills Funding Agency (ESFA) alone now employs 1,800 staff "half as big as the entire education department, and represents a remarkable centralisation of decision-making over school and college funding". Moreover, up until 2010, government equalised funding between rich and poor boroughs but the post-2010 spending cuts of 40% penalised poorer authorities and so poorer people far more than more affluent areas and these cuts have never been undone since. Even today, funding allocations, according to Johnson, are still based on outdated data drawn from censuses and demographic projections dating back to 2013 or even 2000 which "is extraordinary. In fact, it is nothing short of scandalous". As Johnson goes on "This is quite simply a fundamental failure of governance, a failure which slowly, insidiously undermines any rational basis for funding local government and inevitably leads to disillusion, disempowerment, and disengagement." Inevitably people today then feel as they no longer know (or care) what their local council does and certainly don't see local government as the platform for *levelling-up*. A well-educated population is, in Johnson's view, the most vital ingredient in any thriving economy. That starts in the early years, especially supporting the least advantaged. It requires massive investment in schooling with well-trained, well-motivated, properly rewarded teachers. It means "not having an absurdly narrow curriculum" from age 16; having an effective path through (technical) and vocational education and the continued availability of adult education ... . "All this is about the long-term. Policy needs to look to the future(not the past), be consistent and patient, recognise that the benefits may not accrue until well after the next election". While we still have largely a well-functioning state and society in which most people are able to lead a good life, "the warning signs are multiplying" as poverty grows, the welfare safety net frays, our education system fails far too many, especially those from disadvantaged backgrounds and social care is a disaster. "We can, and we must, do better".

Conclusions

Many of the critiques above were neatly and starkly summed up in the House of Lords Select Committee on 11–16 education in England in December 2023; a report that called for "improvement and "urgent change" to address an overloaded curriculum, a disproportionate exam burden and declining opportunities to study creative and technical subjects. "We found that the present system is not adequately equipping young people with the knowledge, skills and behaviours they need to progress to the next phase of their education, and to flourish in the future" with a third of pupils labelled as failures and forgotten. The Committee considered a range of reforms including the idea of a post-16 destination performance measure but it's most incisive and challenging recommendation was that the Government "abandon the EBacc" entirely, the very centre-piece of the current government's education policy and accountability system opening up in the process the opportunity and momentum for a radical rethink of English secondary education in the future; a future that is likely to see a British General Election.

As the Edge Foundation Report in 2018 emphasised, employers now want "well-rounded individuals with the interpersonal skills, resilience and problem-solving abilities that will help them succeed". However, the current system of English education is "actively accelerating in the opposite direction". It attempts "to address the problem of twenty-first century skills using a late nineteenth-century approach to education", while the prioritisation of the Ebacc at the expense of all else has decimated the creative and technical arts at the very time they are the very disciplines employers are calling for. The resultant and exclusive academic offer represents a "great stagnation" in education according to Lynne Rogers and Ken Spours at the UCL Institute of Education (2020), depressing educational attainment, restricting choice and undermining progression. "In the space of a decade, we have moved from a situation where over two-thirds of the cohort could achieve the threshold to move to level 3 study at 16 to one in which this form of progression may now be open (only) to a minority". "GCSE exams are "a relic of the days before the raising of the participation age to 18", totally at odds with the shift internationally to a coherent 14–19 curriculum certified by the International Baccalaureate rather than the binary choice at age 16 in England of HE or Apprenticeships; an economic and social divide that, in their view, the introduction of T-levels will only encourage and reinforce.

School leaders and teachers increasingly agree. According to the 2022 Survey of School Leaders and Teachers by Pearsons, 60% do not think that the current education system is developing tolerant, sustainably minded citizens of the future and 40% do not think that it effectively supports aspiration and achievement. As Sharon Hague, Pearson's Managing Director of School Qualifications (2022) concluded, "it is clear from teachers' responses that collaboration and innovation are key and that the majority of teachers want the education system to evolve to meet the needs of the whole child, equipping children with the skills and confidence they need to adapt to a range of challenges and thrive in adult life". Most particularly "We need to reframe what schools call inclusion-moving away from a traditional model which focuses on the SEND needs of a minority which implicitly messages that 'normal = no needs-to a universal model of inclusion that recognises that' ALL children have learning, wellbeing and safeguarding needs and that every member of staff has a role to play in recognising and responding to them".

Meanwhile, as Britain prepares for a General Election in 2024, Matthew Goodwin (2023) has identified a post-Brexit, post-Covid national mood of apathy and disillusion rather that unity and optimism, a collective sense of hopelessness compounded by ineffectual and dishonest government, a loss of national faith in the now, let alone, in the future as a wave of strikes over pay and conditions sweeps across the UK's public sector, the cost-of-living crisis continues to depress people's incomes and the energy crisis seems to loom large as Britain moves back into the cold and darkness of the winter nights ahead. Or is this just the lull before the storm; the storm of a new General Election and the dawn of a new government committed to radical reform?; a government that might, according to the national study by More in Common (2020) restore common bonds and values, bring Britain back together again as "a country that is hard-working, environmentally friendly, and compassionate". And one where once again "we can disagree and still come together".

The World Learning Crisis

The UK, however, is not alone in facing an existential educational crisis of both policy and practice. Exacerbated and exposed by Covid-19 and the subsequent lockdowns of schools and societies, an international as well as national debate, a global "soul-search" about the future of education, has emerged as governments worldwide search desperately for new solutions to promoting learning in the 21st century; to eliminating or at least mitigating the inequalities that are severely undermining the development of future generations and the future of humankind; a national introspection that has even enveloped mighty America according to the Harvard Leadership Initiative (2014).

The challenges facing the wealthy nations of the Western world, however, are dwarfed by those facing developing countries. As the UNESCO, UNICEF, World Bank Report on The State of Global Learning Poverty in June 2022 declared "The deep pre-Covid learning crisis has been made even more severe by the pandemic" with the Learning Poverty Rate (LPR) rising from 57% in low and middle-income countries in 2019 to an estimated 70% in 2022. The World Bank (2020) calculated that with more than 250 million children are out of primary and secondary school and one-third of those have never been to school, Covid-19 has created a "crisis within a crisis" potentially adding 10% or an additional 72 million school-age children to the LPR and brutally exposing the weaknesses of education systems around the world. The WEF Briefing in April 2020 identified over 1.2 billion children in 186 countries across the world out of the classroom after Covid-19 while the McKinsey & Co. report in April 2022 revealed school closures ranging from 75 weeks or more in Latin America and Southern Asia compared to 30 weeks in Europe and Central Asia; a worldwide *learning crisis* and an expansion of *learning poverty* exacerbated even further by the digital divide in Internet access and use, and in the potential losses in future earnings of some $1.6 trillion worldwide or 0.9% of total global GDP.

However, there are signs of hope on the horizon according to the WEF (2020). Firstly there is a new generation of learners, Generation Alpha, a generation that is no longer steeped in the traditions and confines of 20th-century learning but rather a Generation of 6–18-year-olds who have grown up with new technology and who are as at home in the virtual world of the Internet and their smartphone as they are in the real world at home and in school. They have not seen the world without technology. They have grown up in a globalised world and they have been defined by technology. They work collaboratively, globally and see climate change and mental health as their key priorities. "Generation Alpha, the children of the Millennials, are the most racially diverse generation across the world and one for whom technology is simply an extension of their own consciousness and identity with social media being a way of life". They live within the most non-traditional family structures and according to the WEF, 65% of them will be entering jobs in the future that do not yet exist. Education in the future therefore needs to educate them as citizens of an inter-connected global world, redefining the role of the educator with a shift from knowledge to such life skills as communication, resilience, adaptability and emotional intelligence alongside continuous learning, entrepreneurial skills, creativity and critical skills by unlocking the educational potential of technology.

Secondly, education in the 21st century is no longer a State-only-owned business. It is increasingly becoming yet another Big Tech enterprise; one that may even takeover education as we know it, or result in new forms of state-corporate partnership and regulation. Education is now a trillion-dollar industry that if properly managed may help education leapfrog learning in developing as well as developed countries and so help equip Generation Alpha with "the skills to thrive in tomorrow's world-even if we don't know what it looks like yet"

Whatever else, the 2020–2022 Covid-19 pandemic shook national governments out of their complacency and added fuel to the emerging debate about learning in and for the 21st century; learning not just for the young, not just for the academically ablest but for all ages at all stages throughout life "preparing students for lifelong learning to up-skill and re-skill as adults is key to ensuring they are resilient to mega trends and external shocks" In the era of globalisation, digitalisation and the 100 Year Life, adult learning and training is now as urgent as that for the 3–25 age group, particularly for women and the disadvantaged. The opportunity for fundamental change, for a new educational paradigm for the world at large, is now available but only if the moment is seized and the strategy is developed that takes world education from the 19th and 20th centuries into the 21st century. Such a *Leap of Learning* however will first require the "leap of imagination" needed to fully grasp and grapple with the new context and new challenges ahead and how best to prepare the up-and-coming generations to not only cope with them but overcome them as part of a better world and a better way of life for all humanity.

Bibliography

Altogether Now Report: Inclusion not Exclusion: Supporting All Young People to Succeed at School (April 2022)

Augar Philip: *Post-18 Review of Education and Funding*: Department of Education: (May 2019)

Ball Stephen: The tragedy of state education in England: Reluctance, compromise and muddle-a system in disarray: Sir John Cass Foundation lecture: *Journal of the British Academy*, 6: 207–238 (March 2018)

Bukodi Erzsebet & Goldthorpe John: *Social Mobility and Education in Britain*: C.U.P (2019)

CBI: Learning for Life: Funding a World Class Adult Education System (October 2020)

Centre for Social Justice: Lost & Not Found (March 2023)

Children's Commissioner: 2019 Briefing on "the children leaving school with nothing."

Clarke M: 'Talkin' bout a revolution: the social, political and fantasmatic logics of education policy': *Journal of Education Policy*, 27: 173–191 (2012)

Commission Young Lives: Altogether Now Report: Inclusion not Exclusion: Supporting All Young People to Succeed at School (April 2022)

Coffield F & Williamson B: *From Exam Factories to Communities of Discovery*: Bedford Way Papers (November 2011)

DfE/IPSOS: Employers Survey: Winterbottom M et al. (October 2020)

DfE PISA 2022:National Report for England (Dec. 2023)

DfE: Opportunity for all White Paper (2022)

DfE/ IFF Research & Institute of Education: Working Lives of Teachers and Leaders: Wave 1 (2023)

Duffy B. et al: *Unequal Britain: Attitudes to Inequality after Covid-19*: IFS/Policy Institute/Kings College London (February 2021).

Edge Foundation: Towards a Twenty-First Century Education System (October 2018)

Education Policy Institute (EPI): English Education: World Class?: Andrews J et al (August 2017)

EPI: Education in England: Annual Report: Hutchinson J et al. (August 2020)

EPI: Analysis: GCSE Results Day: Hodge L & Andrews J (August 2023)

EPI: Covid-19 and Disadvantage Gaps in England: Hunt E et al (December 2021)

EPI: Education Recovery and Resilience in England (May 2021)

Fair Education Alliance (FEA): 2022 Report Card: Achieving a Fair Education in England (November 2022)

Farquharson C & McNally S: Education Inequalities: Changes in Education over Time: IFS Deaton Review (August 2022)

Gardner, Howard: Multiple Intelligences: New Horizons in Theory & Practice: Basic Books (2006)

Gillard Derek: Education in England: A History (2018).

Good Childhood Report: The Children's Society (September 2022)

Goodwin Matthew: *Values, Voice and Virtue: The New British Politics*: Penguin (2023)

Green F & Kynaston D: *Britain's Private School Problem: Its Time to Talk*: Guardian (13 January 2019)

Guardian: Levelling-up: Some Wealthy Areas of England to See 10 Times More Funding than Poorest: McIntyre et al (February 2, 2022)

Harvard Advanced Leadership Initiative: Education for the 21st century (August 24–26, 2014)

Hirsh-Pasek Kathy et al: *A New Path to Education Reform: Playful Learning Promotes 21st Century Skills in Schools and Beyond*: Brookings Institute (2020)

House of Commons Education Committee: Special Education Needs and Disabilities (October 2019)

House of Commons Education Committee: A Plan for an Adult Skills and Lifelong Learning Revolution (December 2020)

House of Commons Education Committee: The Future of post-16 Qualifications (April 2023)

House of Lords Select Committee Report: Requires Improvement: Urgent Change for 11-16 Education (December 12, 2023)

Independent Assessment Commission (IAC) Interim Report: The Future of Assessment and Qualifications in England (2021)

Institute of Fiscal Studies (IFS): Annual Report on Education Spending in England (2022)

Institute of Fiscal Studies (IFS): School Spending and Costs: The Coming Crunch (August 2022)

Institute of Fiscal Studies (IFS): Levelling Up (February 2022)

Institute of Government: Schools and coronavirus: The government's handling of education during the pandemic (March 2021)

Institute of Government & Public Policy (IGPP): Launch Your Career Report: Careers after Covid (May 11, 2021)

IPSOS Employers Survey DfE (2019)

Jadhave Cath (Associate Director of Standards & Comparability at Ofqual): Mythbusting: 3 Common Misconceptions (Ofqual Blog: March 17, 2017)

Johnson Paul: *Follow the Money: How Much Does Britain Cost?*: Abacus Books (2023)

Jones, Ken: Education in Britain: Polity Press (2003)

Leading Learner: Rethinking GCSE examinations (September 27, 2020)

Learning Policy Institute(LPI): Reinventing School in the COVID Era and Beyond: Darling-Hammond L et al (September 2020)

Local Government Association (LGA) & Angel Solutions: (LGA): Analysis of Ofsted Inspection Outcomes by School Type: An Analysis Showing That Council-maintained Schools Outperforming Academies (May 2022).

McKinsey & Co: How Covid-19 Caused A Global Learning Crisis (April 4, 2022)

Microsoft: Schools after COVID-19: From a Teaching Culture to a Learning Culture (June 17, 2020)

Monbiot George: *England's Punitive Exam System is Only Good at One Thing: Preserving Privilege*: Guardian (April 27, 2022)

More in Common: Britain's Choice: Common Ground and Division in 2020 s Britain: Juan-Torres et al: (October 2020)

Morris P: An analysis of the 210 schools white paper: *Journal of Education Policy*, 27: 89–107 (2012)

National Audit Office (NAO): Ofsted Inspection of Schools (May 2018)

Newton Paul, Director, Cambridge Assessment Network, Assessment Research & Development: 'A-level pass-rates and the enduring myth of norm-referencing.": Research Matters: UCLES (2011)

NFER study of inspection regimes in six countries-England, Australia, Japan, NZ, Singapore & Wales: What Impact does Accountability have on Curriculum, Standards and Engagement in Education: Frances Brill et al (2018)

OECD International PISA League Table (2018)

OECD: Building Skills For All: A Review of England: Kuczera M et al (2016)

OECD: PISA 2022 Results: Vol. 1 The State of Learning and Equity in Education: Vol. 2: Learning During-and from-Disruption (2023)

Ofsted Annual Report (2022)

Pearson's Survey of School Leaders & Teachers (Schools Today, Schools Tomorrow (June 2022)

Priestland David: Britain's Education System Is Being Tested to Destruction: Opinion: Education Policy (January 13, 2013)

Robinson K & Aronica L: *Creative Schools*: Penguin (2016)

Robinson K & Robinson K: *Imagine IF: Creating a Future for Us All*: Penguin (2022)

Rogers L. and Spours K: The great stagnation of upper secondary education in England: A historical and system perspective: *British Educational Research Journal*, 46(6): 1232–1255 (December 2020)

Royal Society of Arts (RSA): Jobs are Changing, So Should Education (February 2019)

Schleicher Andreas: *The Case for 21st-Century Learning*: OECD (March 2010)

Schleicher Andreas (Director of Education & Skills at the OECD) "the UK is an average performer" quoted in TEC report (May 24, 2021)

Social Mobility Commission 'hotspot-coldspot' analysis in 2017 State of the Nation Report: Social Mobility in Great Britain (November 2017)

Social Mobility Commission: The Long Shadow of Deprivation: Differences in Opportunities Across England (September 2020)

Social Mobility Commission: Against the Odds: Achieving Greater Progress for Secondary Students Facing Socio-economic Disadvantage (2021)

Social Mobility Commission: State of the Nation 2023 (September 2023)

Sutton Trust: Chain Effect (2018)

Sutton Trust & Social Mobility Commission: Elitist Britain (2019)

Sutton Trust: Elites In The UK: Pulling Away? (January 2020)

Sutton Trust: Sutton Trust Cabinet Analysis (2022)

Sutton Trust: Social Mobility-Past, Present and Future (June 2022)

Taylor Jason: Is the British Education System Fit for Purpose in the 21st Century Job Market?: Connections Recruitment (July 18, 2019)

UNICEF: Child-Wellbeing in Rich Countries (Report Card 11) The State of the World's Children (2023)

UNESCO, UNICEF, World Bank: The State of the Global Education Crisis: A Path to Recovery (2021)

UNESCO, UNICEF, World Bank: The State of Global Learning Poverty (June 2022)

UNESCO, UNICEF, World Bank: From Learning Recovery to Education Transformation (September 2022)

UNICEF: Child-Wellbeing in Rich Countries (Report Card 11) The State of the World's Children (2023)

Von Stumm Sophie et al: School quality ratings are weak predictors of students' achievements and well-being: *Journal of Child Psychology and Psychiatry* 62(3): p339–348 (2021)

WEF: COVID-19: What You Need to Know about the Coronavirus Pandemic on 29 April (April 29, 2020)

WEF: 4 ways COVID-19 Could Change How We Educate Future Generations: (March 30, 2020)

West A & Wolfe D: Academies, the School System in England and a Vision for the Future LSE/Matrix Chambers (2018)

Wolf Alison: *Heading for the Precipice: Can Further and Higher Education Funding Policies Be Sustained*: Kings College London (2015)

World Bank: Realizing the Future of Learning Report: From Learning Poverty to Learning for Everyone, Everywhere (December 2020)

World Happiness Report 2023: Helliwell J F et al (March 2023)

Wilkinson D et al: Assessing the Variance in Pupil Attainment: How Important is the School Attended: *National Institute Economic Review*, 243(1): 4–16 (2018)

2   The Global Context and Challenges for Education Today

"We believe that the world is roughly in the middle of a dramatic transition as a result of four fundamental disruptive trends. Any one of these disruptions, by itself, would probably rank among the largest economic forces the global economy has ever seen-including industrial revolutions in advanced economies."
Richard Dobbs et al (2015)

The Global Context of Education

So wrote the Directors of McKinsey Global Institute in 2015, forewarning the emergence of some of the most powerful forces the world has ever seen; forces that would transform the 21st century; forces that would transform education; forces that include globalisation and global inequality; seismic shifts in the world's demography, a paradigm shift in new technology, global warming, global pandemics and the existential future of humankind and the planet. All this alongside tectonic geo-political shifts among the superpowers and the rise of Big-Tech, social media, terrorism and cybercrime; identity politics, populism and the search for *truth*. The world of the 21st century is changing at a rate and in a form that is way beyond our previous experience, and it is operating within a global economy that now stretches across both the developed and the developing worlds, a *polycrisis* whereby individual crises interact and generate a chain-reaction, a "new world disorder" that according to the Ipsos Global Trends (2023) revolves around an economic divide around the future of capitalism as the economic system responsible for creating an environmental crisis and a growing international chasm as people turn to authoritarianism, nationalism and closed borders as defences against both global forces and international migration.

Globalisation

Has clearly been reshaping the *World Economy*. It has integrated the world into a global capitalist system beyond any government control and in the

DOI: 10.4324/9781003358770-3

process created a new breed of "Super-Power", the mega-corporation of the 21st century; and a new breed of global entrepreneur with ambitions of world domination through economic and technological power; power based on the Internet and control of world markets and global finance. In the 21st century, the tech giants Amazon, Apple, Facebook and especially Google see the world as their oysters and they are in the process of creating their own mini-states and centres of power. And behind these *masters of the universe* are waves of new competitors from the developing nations—the "Ali-Babas" of Asia soon to be followed by those from Africa and South America. Meanwhile the Amazon boss, Jeff Bezos, competes with Elon Musk to conquer space; a galactic rivalry that in the past only superpowers like America and the Soviet Union could possibly have afforded.

A new world order is emerging; a Fourth Industrial Revolution according to Klaus Schwab, Director of the WEF (2017), a new global economy and a new generation of entrepreneurs from both the developing and developed nations are challenging, changing and disrupting the global economy in a fight for control of the markets ahead. Not just the real economy as in the past but also the virtual economy identified by researchers such as W. Brian Arthur of McKinsey Associates (2017); a digital economy that through algorithms and various forms of artificial intelligence is creating a new form of business intelligence; an automated form of intelligence and decision making that is external to modern business rather than within it; one that is increasingly rendering human intelligence and decision-making obsolete. Modern computers and software are even now capable of *inter-association*; of communicating amongst themselves, of using their sensors and processors to correlate and interrogate vast banks of data in milliseconds and make sense of patterns that human beings cannot even see. As modern computer systems become increasingly capable of collective communication and decision making independent of human action—then the implications of this shift from internal to external intelligence for the human race as a species are monumental. Autonomous intelligent systems are increasingly capable of taking over the organisation and running of vast swathes of the global economy—from transport and banking through to warfare and healthcare—and transforming them. Jobs may disappear as many fear or simply be transformed and relocated within the virtual economy. Jobs may no longer even be the way that humans earn their living and the 20th-century debate about the creation of wealth may shift to a 21st-century debate about the distribution of wealth. This would represent a shift from an economic debate to a political debate; one about what on one hand is just and fair and on the other about what the planet can sustain; a debate between the free market philosophy of the USA, the more collectivist style of government found in Europe and the State capitalism practised in China and elsewhere as the tectonic plates underpinning the world balance of power begin to shift from the democratic West to the autocratic East; from America and Europe to China and Asia.

Such hyper-globalisation, however, also seems to be creating a world where human beings feel increasingly insecure, isolated and left behind and one that has stimulated an anti-globalisation backlash and a surge in distrust of national governments reflected in Britain's Brexit vote, and in Donald Trump's US election in 2016. Whole communities feel overwhelmed and powerless against the pace and impact of global change, and of global migration, on themselves and their communities. As a consequence, they distrust the liberal elites in capital cities who have run their countries since 2008; they are instinctively nationalist in outlook and highly sceptical of global change. The post-war structures of largely western leadership are tottering and adopting almost a siege mentality in trying to cope with the new global forces banging on their door and although the election of Joe Biden, after the turbulence of Donald Trump's US presidency, helped restore calm to world leadership, the outcome of the US presidential election in 2024 and the ongoing war in Ukraine—and now in Gaza—may soon test western leadership and unity to the limit and allow the rising powers of the East to take over. We now live in what the McKinsey Global Institute (January 2019) has called "an era of disruption": a disruption that is intensifying, exacerbating the *Digital Divide*, polarising global inequality more starkly and overtly and "splintering" the long-held social contracts that have kept business, the economy and society bound together.

New Technology and the Internet

Are clearly at the heart of this transformation and of *Life in the 21st Century*, transforming world communication and generating revolutions of their own; revolutions of interconnectivity, virtual reality and cyberspace previously unheard of and undreamt of; revolutions in science and technology that will transform human life and both the way we live and how long we live. Artificial intelligence and the rise of the robot have the potential to transform working life and the world economy; biotechnology to transform our bodies and how long we live; algorithms to transform our financial world and the power of global corporations to know us better than we know ourselves, predict our inner secrets and control the way we live, vote and buy. The Internet of Things, the growth of Big Data and the proliferation of data collecting devices and data services all round us, from GPS, CCTV and physical sensors in our cities and on our roads through to the explosion in market intelligence about what we buy, what we want, what we think and how we behave is creating a *data revolution*. It is creating "game-changing" opportunities for businesses, big and small, to satisfy our every need, our every whim-even before we know it. It is transforming not only modern manufacturing and retail but impacting on every other sector too-even the "weather of things". New technology is already part of human life; robots are already here and working amongst us (Danny Fortson: October 2022); invisible through all sorts of surveillance and data systems; visible in the form of the mechanical robots now "slaving away" in factories around the world, in the delivery bots buzzing around the streets of Milton Keynes in the UK or the humanoid robots politely serving clients as receptionists or waitresses in many of Japan's hotels today. *Sofia* has now demonstrated that humanoid robots are as adept at answering questions in media interviews as any politician (YouTube); and *Ai-Da*, the world's first humanoid artist, has already had her self-portrait on show at the London Design School and an interview with both the House of Lords and the *Sunday Times* (July 30, 2023). "I create art that expresses and explores the human experience, so that in a sense, it has soul, even though I do not have one"; and she can tell jokes such as "why did the robot sneeze? Because it caught a virus". The real "game-changer" though is likely to be the advent of Generative AI with ChatGPT and GitHub Copilot making huge headlines and huge profits as AI advances from simple data patterning to creating original content from existing data "taking technology into realms previously thought to be reserved for humans". With Generative AI, computers can now arguably exhibit creativity in the form of blogs, articles and essays, create computer code and "even theorize on the reason for a production error." And AI is already infiltrating such traditionally creative fields as marketing, engineering, risk analysis and R&D. Generative AI is here to stay according to Michael Chui and colleagues at McKinsey & Co (Dec. 2022) and AI innovation is already becoming a "Superpower Steeplechase" according to the *Sunday Times* (October 2021) with the UK currently ranked 3rd in Tortoise Media's Global AI Index behind USA and China but only 19th in terms of AI infrastructure and 11th in terms of AI development. Ironically, AI is also putting Big-Tech itself under siege and according to Danny Fortson (January 2023) Google's dominance of the Internet search engine market is now under threat from Apple and Amazon and a host of new comers using Open AI and Large Language Models (LLMs) from Anthropic and Cohere to A121 and Adept. Market competition seems about to achieve what legislators across the world couldn't do in breaking the Google-Facebook stranglehold on the world-wide web. Such market competition, however, is limited to the very small number of companies and countries capable of funding such transformative innovation and meanwhile as Azeem Azhar

(2022) has argued the rest of humankind is being left behind. Eight of the world's top ten richest companies are tech-based creating a new *economic aristocracy* with the power and resources to transform the future and propel the shifts to the green economy of solar power, genetic engineering and quantum physics; a role previously only the State could have afforded. Ironically, amid all today's high-tech wizardry, the Internet itself, the world-wide web that binds the world of the 21st century together, is extremely fragile and under strain. It was "not so much invented as cobbled together from spare parts and quick fixes" According to James Ball (October 2021) it is extremely vulnerable to underwater cable breakages, clumsy user mistakes or online attacks or viruses while many of the online payment and communication systems using the Net are based on databases compiled in the 1970s using Cobol, a computer language no longer used. More worrying too, AI is now identified as an existential threat to the human race itself. As writers such as Kathryn Parsons have argued (Sunday Times: April 2023), it cannot be trusted. It has its "flaws". It apparently hallucinates, occasionally presenting false or even made-up information; it is occasionally "a bit evil" giving advice on money laundering, writing threatening letters and creating ways to create toxic toxins. AI has no moral compass, and no set of values. AI cannot determine *truth*; it makes mistakes and has inbuilt bias. It can imitate or impersonate a given person, product or style but not, currently at least, apparently be funny or do original research. Huge questions therefore arise about who owns and who controls AI and for what purpose; concerns that have led to a growing critique of AI regarding it ambitions, ownership and ultimately, its part in the world. Leading figures such as Stephen Hawking, Elon Musk and now even AI's Founding Father, Geoffrey Hinton, have all warned that AI is now "humanity's greatest threat" and that we are in danger of becoming what Josh Glancy (February 2023) referred to as an "Algocracy" a society ruled by algorithms. The even greater worry is that AI becomes part of a new "arms race"; an arms race in which cyber warfare will be as key as military combat, when millions of cheap nuclear armed drones descend on enemy cities? Certainly, the Internet has its *Dark Side*, a Wild West that Yuval Harari (2015) described as "a free and lawless zone that erodes state sovereignty, ignores borders, abolishes privacy and poses perhaps the most formidable global security risk". Organised crime has thrived on the "dark net" while terrorists have "weaponised" social media in recruiting new members and waging global jihad. Meanwhile, *Big Data*—your personal details and preferences—is being harvested by virtually every company that we now deal with and sold onto others in an open market whilst GPS and CCTV mean that every move we make can be monitored and tracked. *Big Brother* is alive and very well in the world of the 21st century with Google and Facebook watching our every move and predicting the next one. Amazon has even managed to persuade us to install Alexa in our homes not just as a voice-box but as a "family friend". Data protection is becoming a hope rather than a reality and at times, even these Tech Giants do not seem to be in control of their own content let alone governments or parents. Fake news and post-truth seem to have taken over objective reporting and debate with terrorist and foreign security organisations using social media to distort political elections and even young minds. "Big lies" are now much easier to communicate than "Big Truths" and *Big Government* seems increasingly unable to control, let alone tax the Tech Giants whilst the social and psychological repercussions of their activities on human communication and social relationships are only just beginning to emerge. While the smartphone is a miraculous invention, it has generated a whole new economic system designed to exploit people's human vulnerability and hold their attention 24/7. While Mark Zuckerberg's original grand vision of Facebook might have been that it would open up human connectivity across the world, many observers now see it as having helped create a more anti-social and inward-looking global society as texting and Facebook become a 21st-century addiction that has not only intruded into people's homes but into their children's minds. As Frank Foer (2018) has asked, have these Tech Giants become a new form of world power or worse a new form of tyranny and in the process, begun to distort, if not derail democracy, as it is claimed happened in the 2016 American Presidential election. Are we sleep-walking into a world where "we're constantly watched and constantly distracted" Is the whole world now sliding towards "info-tyranny" as smart technology spreads and becomes more sophisticated? As Ronald J. Deibert (2021) has highlighted corporate power now rests on the "unprecedented and extraordinary visibility of everyone's personal lives right down to the genetic and possibly sub-conscious levels"; levels we all collude in and happily submit to apparently blithely unaware of its potential consequences. Technology that according to Kai Strittmatter (2019), the Chinese Government is now systematically using to create the perfect "Surveillance State"; a colourful mix of George Orwell's (1984), Aldous Huxley's *Brave New World* and Steven Spielberg's Minority Report based ultimately on self-surveillance through new technology; a new Social Contract whereby in return for ever-growing economic prosperity, 1.4 billion Chinese citizens submit to having every one of their actions and transactions recorded through their smartphones so that in effect they are willingly self-censoring and self-sanctioning themselves. And being rewarded or sanctioned by a State that not only knows what all its citizens are doing at any one time but that through its algorithms can potentially predict what they are likely to do in the future; particularly those who may express dissent or opposition to the

State or Communist Party. Hence too, the growing fear in many western nations that companies like Huawei and TikTok are not independent enterprises but arms of the Chinese state and that increasingly Chinese students abroad are not independent learners but agents of the Chinese Communist Party (CCP) sending sensitive western research findings back to the Motherland. The WEF (2017) now has AI and Robotics amongst its Top Ten Global Risks while Stephen Hawking predicted in his final publication (2018) that "Creating AI would be the biggest event in human history. Unfortunately, it might also be the last unless we can learn how to avoid the risks"; a conclusion that has now led Professor Stuart Russell (2023), the godfather of AI, to call for a "kill switch" to be built into all AI to prevent it breaking out of human control. Mustafa Suleyman (2023), the co-founder of DeepMind, in turn, is now warning that for all the huge potential benefits of AI in synthetic biology and other fields, the dangers of drone terrorism, bio-engineered super viruses and cyber-attacks are now so great that they may lead to techno-dictatorships such as China or to "hezbollahization" as the world splinters into regional techno-wars that only governments and international treaties can contain. As Matthew Syed commentated in the *Sunday Times* (May 14, 2023) "our species has made us powerful beyond imagination but also acutely vulnerable" not only to climate change, new technology and geo-political conflict but also because we seem to be living in "a state of denial" between "the seriousness of our predicament and the shallowness of our culture". We may have the intelligence to deal with these questions but do we have the wisdom. As EO Wilson argued "The real problem of humanity is that we have palaeolithic emotions, medieval institutions and godlike technology. It's terrifically dangerous. It's now approaching a point of crisis overall".

Future Work and Employment

According to the WEF Future of Jobs Survey (October 21, 2020), 50% of all employees will need reskilling by 2025, and "half of us will need to reskill in the next five years" while the 2023 Deloitte Global Human Capital Trends Survey concluded that today's models of work have no future. The future is one of new frontiers and a borderless and boundless landscapes in which old assumptions and structures are being challenged and disrupted or cast aside and new ideas, innovations and business models are flooding in and being reimagined. Current organisations no longer control the future but are part of the evolutionary race to the next economic platform; to the Next Heights of Industry in which employee-worker collaboration will be key in unlocking human talent, harnessing worker agency, focusing on global risk and prioritising human outcomes over shareholder profit, sustainability and greater equality. A Brave New World of infinite possibilities but existential dangers for which leaders today seem unprepared and ill-equipped according to this survey. The Age of Man (Anthropocene), therefore, seems to be giving way to the Age of the Machine (Technocene), to what Brynjolfsson and McAfee (2014) once called a Second Machine Age; an age where machines can think for themselves and develop their own network of communication; an age where the Genome and the DNA Revolution are raising not only the prospect of DNA editing to cut out rogue genes but creating CRISPR, the means to redesign life itself. The Covid-19 pandemic totally disrupted global work and life and both exposed and accelerated such underlying trends as remote working and learning, the adoption of new technology and the work polarisation between high and low-skill workers, forcing governments, companies and people to seriously rethink their priorities notably about public and personal health, their way of life and personal relationships, their future prospects and impending risks. As the WEF highlighted in its 2017 Global Human Capital Report managing the future of work will require an education revolution not just for the young but for the old too. As the ILC-UK (2020) has argued, to maximize the Longevity Dividend now emerging across most of the G20 countries, older people aged 50-69 will increasingly need to become the majority of the workforce and the drivers of whole new silver markets in health, transport, housing and recreation as well as creating a vast new volunteer workforce.

Ageing and the Demographic Shift towards the 100-Year Life

Globalisation and the 4th Industrial Revolution, however, are not working in isolation. Beneath the economic and political surface, the world is undergoing a silent revolution; a demographic revolution that is reshaping human society, its nature and its structure. "**By 2030** the world's population is projected to rise by more than 1 billion bringing the total to over eight billion.97% of this population growth will come from emerging or developing countries. Equally significantly, people in all regions are living longer and having fewer children. The result is that the fastest growing segment of the population will be the over 65s-there will be 390 million more of them in 2030 than in 2015"(PWC: 2020).

The world has already reached 8 billion as we all live longer-much longer. Globally life expectancy at birth, according to the UN 2019 *World Population Prospects* Report, is projected to rise from 72.6 years in 2019 to 77.1 by 2050—an astonishing rise of nearly five years; a rise of nearly 13 years in all since 1990. **By 2050,** there will be more older people aged 65 and above in the world than children and young people aged 15–24 years. By 2100, 23%—nearly a quarter- of the world's population—is projected to be aged 65 and over with the *oldest old*, those aged 80 years and over, projected to more than triple from 143 million in 2019 to 426 million in 2050; and then double again to 881 million by 2100; a 16-fold increase in just over 100 years and nearly 10% of the world's population at the beginning of the 22nd century. By the middle of the century, China alone could have a third of its population over the age of 60 and up to 100 million people over 80 years of age; a phenomenal increase from the 14 million 80-year-olds on the entire planet only a century ago.

But world populations are not only exploding with older people but "imploding" as their younger populations shrink through fertility rates so low that they no longer replace the older ages dying out. There will, therefore, soon be an explosion of "**super-aged**" nations, those with 20% or more of their population aged 65 or older, from 3 in 2013 to 34 in 2030 with countries such as Russia, Germany, Greece, Italy and even China now part of what you what George Magnus (2009) has rather dramatically called "the demographic death row" as their populations "implode" and shrink. The potential impact of Global Ageing is profound and as the UN predicted in 2012, potentially permanent and all-pervasive affecting every aspect of society. By 2050, Japan, the world's oldest nation may "have almost as many dependents as working age adults. No society has seen such a thing before" (Economist:2020 study) And, as Paul Hewitt predicted back in 2004: "We are going to see the decline of Europe and Japan as economic powers … as the economies of the West start to shrink and the economies of the emerging markets rise" with the "younger" nations of Asia and Africa outgrowing the superpowers of America, Russia and China. Nigeria, for example, is set to explode demographically from 57 million to 374 million by 2050 and India is predicted to replace China as the most populous country in the world with a projected population of some 1.6 billion people. A global generation gap is therefore emerging as the developed nations age and the poorer countries become adolescent on a scale and at a speed never seen before: "In 1950, the difference in the median age between Japan and Yemen, the worlds' oldest and youngest countries, was just 2.7 years. Today it's about 27 years, and by 2025 it will be 35 years". It is in the very young and often very poor countries such as Iraq, Yemen and Afghanistan where civil conflict is rife and the typical person is a teenager. As Paul Hewitt (2002) put it, if you want to know where the worlds' future conflicts are likely to be "look at the youthful countries".

So, over the next 30 years, the World is potentially facing a *demographic double whammy*; a simultaneous Population Explosion of both Young and Old; a demographic revolution that will in turn have a fundamental impact on the global economy creating whole new markets; new silver markets and silver cities seeking to serve the explosion of older people around the world. In the view of the McKinsey Report on Urbanisation Global Consumers in 2016 *"The developed retiring and elderly will be extraordinarily important to global consumption from 2015 to 2030"*, generating \$4.4 trillion and accounting for nearly 60% of consumption growth in Western Europe and North East Asia alone; an age-shift in global consumption that, however, can only be executed harmoniously if ageing operates in partnership with new technology to offset the catastrophic falls in the dependency ratios predicted for 2030 and beyond. Germany's working population, for example, is projected by the European Commission to shrink from 54 million to 36 million by 2060 with cataclysmic results for its economy and its people, especially the young. Japan is already at the 'spearhead' of this *demographic nightmare*, investing heavily in a Robot Revolution that it hopes will revive its stagnant economy and liberate the millions of ageing people in danger of being left dependent and isolated. (*Guardian*: January 23, 2023)

And behind this tectonic shift in demography lies an accelerating global migration as people from the war-torn and poorer nations flood across continents desperate for peace and prosperity in the wealthier west. As Ben Judah (June 2023) explains "Europe is changing before our eyes" as wave after wave of migrants seek refuge and freedom and generate enormous political and economic tensions alongside fundamental moral ones; an epochal shift as Africa and Asia merge into Europe while "Fortress Europe" attempts to keep them out by blockades or segregate them through discrimination. Migrant populations are growing across Europe and the World Bank estimates that by 2050 216 million refugees could be on the move with huge implications for the economy, politics and social fabric of recipient nations (see also Paul Morland's Human tide 2019 and IOM (UN Migration) World Migration Report 2022).

Urbanisation

Meanwhile, while ageing is reshaping the demography of the world, urbanisation is reshaping its *Geography*, sweeping away traditional ways of life and instigating a tidal shift of human populations from the country to the city in numbers and at a pace never seen before in developing countries. As the World Urbanization Prospects Report (2019) declared "The future of the world's population is urban" *and by 2050* "roughly two thirds (68%) of the world's population will be living in urban areas" as some 3 million people a week move from villages to towns and cities. Nearly 90% of this spatial shift is likely to be concentrated in Asia and Africa whilst megacities of over 10 million inhabitants are set to grow from 33 in 2018 to between 41 and 53 by 2030 as the emerging economies of China, India and Nigeria grow and expand. These megacities are becoming the nerve centres of a global economy that is fast beyond the control of national or even international government. They now control "nearly half of global GDP growth" (McKinsey 2016) and according to the 2019 Global Cities Index, generate intense city-state competition for people and business as western giants such as London, New York and Paris face growing pressure from eastern challengers such as Beijing, Shanghai and Mumbai and—in recent years—an influx of *Silver Surfers* as Baby boomers world-wide seek urban life-styles in later life.

Inequality and Social Mobility

Covid-19, however, did not only speed up the development of technology. It accelerated global and national inequality. According to the Credit Suisse Research Institute's 2021 Global Wealth Report, total global wealth actually increased during the pandemic by 7.4% and ironically, the countries most affected by Covid gained the most, mainly as a result of massive transfers from the public purse to households and businesses given the exceptionally low-interest rates world-wide. 1.1% of the world's population now collectively own $191.6 trillion or 46% of all global wealth while the bottom 55%, some 2.9 bn people, own a mere $5.5 trillion or 1.3%. The world's ten richest men alone now own more wealth than the bottom 40% of the world's population while Elon Musk, for example, apparently pays only 3.2% at a "true tax rate" and Jeff Bezos less than 1%. This escalating inequality has inevitably reignited the Global Wealth Tax Debate and on June 5, 2023, the G7 finance ministers agreed to an historic 15% minimum global corporate tax rate and a guaranteed share of taxes for countries on the profits of large multi-national corporations. Oxfam and others, however, want to go further, much further and in its Survival of the Fittest report (January 16, 2023) Oxfam argued that "A tax of up to 5% on the world's multi-millionaires and billionaires could raise $1.7 trillion a year, enough to lift 2 billion people out of poverty and fund a global plan to end hunger"; while in the UK, the charity Autonomy is planning to run trials on the benefits of a Universal Basic Income (UBI) of £1600 per month to combat accelerating poverty. However, as Tom Calver has highlighted (February 2023) inequality isn't only about wealthy individuals, families or even social classes. With accelerating longevity, it is increasingly about what happens when wealthy generations such as the Boomer Generation begin to pass on their wealth to their Millennial children and grand-children, Generations X, Y and Z. The Fourth Industrial Revolution according to the WEF's Global Social Mobility Report 2020 (January 2020) has brought greater benefits in "raising the living standards of billions and lifting millions out of poverty", but it has equally exacerbated a growing sense of unfairness, precarity, perceived loss of identity and dignity, weakening social trust in institutions, disenchantment with political processes, and an erosion of the traditional social contract. The 2020 WEF Social Mobility Index, for example, showed the Nordic countries and parts of Europe outperforming the rest of the world, but the UK was ranked only 21st and the USA 27th out of the 82 countries surveyed. Inequality across the world is now so gross and glaring that as the UN (2020) has passionately warned "a sustained reduction in inequality" is now desperately needed if the world is not to split apart.

Climate Change

Is clearly now becoming a, if not *the* top global emergency; one described by the UN in April 2022 as "a fast-track to disaster" unless drastic and immediate action is taken to limit global warming to 1.5 degrees. However, as Cath Everett (Dec. 2022) has argued "There is no credible way to prevent the planet from experiencing a devastating and irreversible temperature increase" above the net-zero figure of 1.5% above pre-industrial levels set by the UN's 2015 Paris Agreement for 2050 despite the US Inflation Reduction Act being described as "the most significant legislation in history to tackle the climate crisis" According to the MGI report (January 2022), the cost of the transition to net-zero would be immense and it would need to be universal. It would represent economic transformation costing an estimated \$275 trillion over the 30 years to 2050, a rise of \$3.5 trillion on capital spending currently. It would hit some communities and sectors harder than others and as the war in Ukraine has dramatically illustrated, it would expose dramatic inequalities in access to resources. Even the transition to a Green Economy requires scarce materials and right now according to Yeomans and Harter (May 2022) China "Owns the earth" and controls most of the minerals critical to the modern and future green economy, notably in Central Africa; precious metals such as nickel, cobalt, copper and lithium essential to electrification, batteries and the green revolution and while the West is seeking ways to fight back through alternative sources, technologies and recycling, they are still way behind. As Ben Judah (2023) has aptly argued, the fossil age of the first industrial revolution is giving way to the mineral age of the green revolution-an energy and mineral shift in economic wealth that, in turn, will generate a geo-political shift of monumental proportions as governments and corporations scour the earth and the seas for new resources. So, the Green Revolution is not just an economic and technological revolution. Potentially, it represents a new stage in human evolution and humankind's relationship to both its environment and to each other. The free market capitalist model of economic growth and material wellbeing has generated and legitimised the untrammelled and rapacious exploitation of people and the planet bringing humankind to the cliff-edge of extinction. In the view of many authorities, it is no longer a sustainable model of economic development and its metric of GDP is no longer a sustainable model of national wealth (Sunday Times/ Raconteur 17–10 2021) It measures the value of goods and services created in a country over a set period. It does not, however, measure unrealised assets or asset depreciation or the quality of life in terms of "peace, quality of education, mental health or the protection on natural capital needed for our survival" Rather GDP encourages unfettered material consumption and totally ignores the costs of growth and the damage that the exploitation of both people and nature involves. In the author's view, we need a new model of economic development, a green model with possibly a green measure of GDP if the humankind is to find a more sustainable and renewable relationship with nature. Moreover, both climate change and Russia's invasion of Ukraine and the subsequent Cost-of-Living Crisis have vividly reminded us of how crucial *Energy* is to life on Planet Earth and how it is becoming increasingly scarce. As Matthew Syed has argued (September 2022), energy is both the engine of economic growth and the future of productivity "We must (therefore) put energy at the heart of everything we think and do" and generate a paradigm change in personal thinking and economic policy-making under the mantra *Energy, Energy, Energy*. Unfortunately, according to the Climate Change Committee Progress Report (2023), the UK lags badly behind and now threatens to go even slower having moved its deadline for banning new petrol and diesel cars from 2030 to 2035. "Change has been incremental at best and key policies delayed".

Geo-Political Shift

And amid all the global megatrends above, there lurks a tectonic shift in the world's *balance of power*; a shift represented by Russia's invasion of Ukraine for territory and China's ambition for economic and technological supremacy. The International Relations Report (2023) identifies seven geo-political shifts likely to change the international world, shifts that include the changing relationships between the rising and declining superpowers, all nuclear armed following the decline of the USA, Russia, Europe and Japan and the rise of China and India; rising tensions with independence movements within such nations as Palestine, Kurdistan, Myanmar and the UK alongside the rising tensions between superpowers over such contested areas as South China Seas and Ukraine. Tensions too are rising rapidly over the causes and the victims of climate change between developed and developing nations while the weakness of the UN due to the power of the single vote veto within the Security Council is badly undermining its ability to lead, resolve and even referee global conflicts and implement global solutions.

The choice, as Richard Fisher (2023) has indicated, is between long-term and forward planning and the short-termism of many democratic governments; *a tyranny of the instant* driven by media headlines, 5-year election cycles and capitalism's need for quick profits rather than long-term investments. Today's problems are passed onto future generations, the world is fragmenting into spheres of influence while global decision making is often hidden behind "closed doors" antagonising public opinion and generating a dangerous gulf between national, short-term solutions and long-term global needs. Reforming the UN will be a critical first step or else "the world will become guilty of a terrible derelictions of duty" to humanity at large. Democratic nations not only face competition from authoritarian governments but from global corporations; corporations with transnational power to control governments as well as global markets and with AI as their new ally in subtly controlling consumer mentality as well as their behaviour. As the UK's Ministry of Defence Report (2018) concluded "The only certainty about the future is its inherent uncertainty" in a world that desperately needs greater human empowerment not powerlessness and international structures capable of managing or at least mitigating potential conflict, of regulating the rise of the Tech Titans and MNPs and social media, and guiding the economic and societal transformations currently underway as new technology alongside increasing environmental stress and the demographic shifts of ageing, emerging young nations and mass migration increasingly shape a future where *unknowns increasingly outweigh knowns* and black swans, black jellyfish and human "blind spots" proliferate as politicians fail to spot or respond to the forces before them. And behind so much of these shift lies China's ambitions as a global superpower; an ambition sheathed in stealth as much as in threat; an international take-over conducted through investment rather than war as described by Robert Watts and Jamie Nimo (Sunday Times: January 2023) while Ian William's book *The Fire of the Dragon: China's New Cold War* (2022) is a chilling description of China's secret army of cyber spies and patriotic hackers employed to undermine democratic societies, steal data, censor content and generate an alternative pro-China narrative via such apparently innocent social media websites as TikTok. And such subversive infiltration is not limited to China. As Robert Watts argued previously (Sunday Times March 6, 2022) the infiltration by Russian oligarchs across the UK and especially in London has been just as insidious and widespread, and MI6 is increasingly concerned now about assassins from Iran seeking revenge on enemies in the UK.

Conclusion

The Global World of the 21st century, therefore, now seems like one of "cascading catastrophes" that through "error or terror" will send shock-waves across the planet. Globalisation appears to be outstripping itself, outstripping the globe's sustainability and threatening the very survival of humankind and the planet. As Josh Glancy has argued (February 27, 2022). "We are living, it seems, in an age of permanent crisis; stumbling blindly from one calamity to the next, scrolling anxiously through phone alerts and Twitter threads, trying to make sense of the latest Very Bad News". Political policies on health, education, housing and transport abound but "they are each debated and analysed in narrow little silos driven by short-term needs with no common strategy or coherent vision". And after the vaudeville of Conservative politicians in the UK in recent years, "we need a new breed of leader"; not the showmen and publicists but the synthesisers capable of seeing and communicating the long-term national interest and pursuing it effectively. The current British political system encourages instant solutions and short-term fixes rather than long-term analyses with ministers in office for months rather than years and governments driven by election deadlines, media headlines and factional infighting rather than the public interest. As the futurologist Blair Sheppard commented (Nov. 26, 2020), the crises of the next 10 years—economic, environmental, technological, governmental—are so profound and toxic as to forewarn a possible collapse of human civilisation. There is a breakdown in the post-war global consensus leading to a world fractured by nationalism, and populism with trust and the loss of confidence in traditional institutions and authorities at an all-time low. The world of the 21st century needs new leadership and new types of leader, institutions need a fundamental rethink about their purpose and way of working so that they can reconnect with ordinary people and regain their trust; and any political strategy needs to start with a Local-Mindset as a first step so that people can see and feel change around them not thousands of miles away. Traditional methods of decision making and execution are no longer fit for the purposes and speed needed.

So, in the face of such overwhelming global issues, how does education possibly prepare young people for such fundamental and existential questions and for their future life as individuals, families, workers and citizens when the planet and the world we live in seems to be in such a state of flux and perpetual crisis? Does education therefore now need a fundamental transformation, a fundamental rethink as to its purpose and design, its mission and ambition; a search that is explored next in Chapter 3, if there is to be any hope of saving the world and saving the future generations living in it.

Bibliography

Ai-Da: *A Life in the Day (of) Ai-Da*: Sunday Times Magazine (July 30, 2023)

Arthur W. Brian: *The Second Economy*: McKinsey Quarterly (2017)

Azhar Azeem: *How Accelerating Technology is Leaving Us Behind and What to Do About It*: Random House Business (2022)

Baldwin Richard: *The Globotics Upheaval: Globalization, Robotics and the Future of Work*: W&N (2019)

Ball James: The Vulnerability of the Internet Sunday Times (October 10, 2021)

Brynjolfsson Erik & McAfee Andrew: *The Second Machine Age*: W.W. Norton & Co. (2014)

Brynjolfsson Erik & McAfee Andrew: *Machine, Platform, Crowd-Harnessing Our Digital Future*: W.W. Norton (2017)

Calver Tom: *The Age of Inheritocracy*: Sunday Times (February 19, 2023)

Chui Michael et al: *Generative AI is here*: McKinsey (December 20, 2022)

Climate Change Committee (UK): Progress in adapting to climate change: 2023 Report to Parliament (March 2023)

Credit Suisse Research Institute: Global Wealth Report 2021 (June 2021)

Deibert Ronald J: *Reclaiming the Internet for Civil Society*: September Publishing (2021)

Deloitte Global Human Capital Trends Survey: *New fundamentals for a boundaryless world*: Deloitte Insights (January 9, 2023)

Dobbs R, Manyika J, Woetzel J: *No Ordinary Disruption*: Public Affairs/Perseus (2015)

Economist The: Franklin, D & Andrews, J: 2020 Report (2012)

Everett Cath: *Clear and present danger (of climate change)*: Sunday Times/Raconteur (December 18, 2022)

Fisher Richard: *The Long View: Why We Need to Transform How the World Sees Time*: Wildfire (2023)

Foer Frank: *World Without Mind*: Penguin/Random House (2018)

Fortson Danny: The Robot Revolution is Already Here: Sunday Times (ST) (October 2, 2022)

Fortson Danny: *AI is Coming to Steal Your Face*: Sunday Times (December 5, 2021)

Fortson Danny: *The Search Revolution Threat to Tech Giants' Domination*: Sunday Times (January 1, 2023)

Fortson Danny: *The Chat GTP Revolution is Real*: Sunday Times (February 5, 2023)

Fortson Danny: *5 ways AI Will Change All Our Lives*: Sunday Times (February 12, 2023)

Glancy Josh: *We are Living it Seems in an Age of Permanent Crisis*: Sunday Times News Review (February 27, 2022)

Glancy Josh: *We are in Danger of Becoming an "Algocracy" a Society Ruled by Algorithms*: Sunday Times Magazine (February 2023)

Global Ageing Council on Ageing Society: *Global Population Ageing: Peril or Promise?*: WEF (2012)

Global Cities Index (2019)

Goodhart David: *The Road to Somewhere*: Penguin (2017)

Guardian: Japan's Ageing Population Poses Urgent Risk to Society (January 23, 2023)

Harari Yuval Noah: *Homo Deus: A Brief History of Tomorrow*: Penguin/Vintage Books (2015)

Hawking Stephen: *Brief Answers to the Big Questions*: John Murray (2018)

Hewitt P: *Global Aging and the Rise of the Developing World*: Geneva Papers, Vol. 27, pp.477–485 (2002).

ILC-UK: Health Equals Wealth: the Global Longevity Dividend (October 2020)

International Relations Report: Geopolitics and International relations-Possibilities 2050: The Future of the World (2023)

IOM (UN Migration): *World Migration Report* (2022)

Ipsos: Global Trends (2023)

Judah Ben: "To succeed in the electric era, dig yourself a mine": Sunday Times (September 3, 2023)

Kearney: Global Cities Report & Index: A question of talent (2019)

Longman P: *Think Again: Global Aging*: Foreign Policy News (October 12, 2010)

Magnus George: *The Age of Ageing*: John Wiley & Sons (2009)

McKinsey Global Institute(MGI): Urbanisation and Global Consumers (2016)

McKinsey Global Institute(MGI: *Navigating a World of Disruption*: Briefing Note for WEF (January 2019)

McKinsey Global Institute (MGI): *The Social Contract in the 21st Century* (February 2020)

McKinsey & Co: "On the cusp of a new era? (October 2020)

McKinsey Global Institute (MGI): *Covid-19 has Revived the Social Contract in Advanced Economies-for Now* (December 2020)

McKinsey & Co: The future of Work after COVID-19 (February 18, 2021)

McKinsey Global Institute (MGI): The Net-Zero Transition: What it Would Cost, What it Could Bring (January 2022)

McKinsey & Company: Reversal of Fortune: How European Software Can Play To Its Strengths (February 17, 2022)

Morland Paul: *The Human Tide*: John Murray (2019)

Oxfam: Survival of the Fittest (January 16, 2023)

Oxfam: Profiting from Pain (May 23, 2022)

Parsons Kathryn: *ChatGPT Heralds a Productivity Leap Beyond Our Wildest Dreams*: Sunday Times (April 2, 2023)

PWC: *Demographic and Social Change* (2020)

PWC: Workforce of the Future: The Competing Forces Shaping 2030 (2018)

Russell Stuart: *Human Compatible*: Penguin (2023)

Schwab Klaus: *The Fourth Industrial Revolution*: Crown Publishing Group (2017)

Sheppard Blair: *10 Years to Midnight*: Penguin Random House (2020)

Social Mobility Commission: Social Mobility Barometer 2021 (March 11, 2021)

Strittmatter Kai: *We Have Been Harmonised*: Old Street Publishing (2019)

Suleyman Mustafa, with Bhaskar Michael: *The Coming Wave: AI and the 21st Century's Greatest Dilemma*: Bodley Head (2023)

Sunday Times/ Raconteur: Superpowered Steeplechase: A Scramble for AI Supremacy (October 24, 2021)

Sunday Times/ Raconteur: GDP and its Inadequacy as a Measure of National Wealth (17–10 2021)

Sunday Times Rich List (2021 and 2023)

Syed Matthew: *Powerful Beyond Imagination But Also Acutely Vulnerable*: Sunday Times (May 14, 2023)

Syed Matthew: *Energy is Both the Engine of Economic Growth and the Future of Productivity*: Sunday Times (September 25, 2022)

Toffler Alvin: Future Shock: Turtleback Books (1970)

Tsang Steve: *Xi's Student Spy Army-and How They can be Outsmarted*: Sunday Times (August 27, 2023)

UK's Ministry of Defence Report: *Global Strategic Trends*: The Future Starts Today (Sixth Edition: 2018)

UNO (Dept. of Economic and Social Affairs: Population Division): *World Population Prospects Report* (2019)

UNO (DESA): *World Urbanization Prospects Report* (2019)

UNO(DESA): Inequality in a Rapidly Changing World (2020)

UNO: Climate Change Annual Report 2022 (April 2022)

UNO(DESA): *Leaving No One Behind In An Ageing World*: World Social Report (2023)

Watts Robert: *The Deep Roots of the Russian Money Tree*: Sunday Times (Mar. 6 2022)

Watts Robert & Nimo Jamie: *China's £150 bn BITE OUT of Britain*: Sunday Times (January 1, 2023)

White Olivia: *How Our Interconnected World is Changing*: McKinsey Podcast: (February 9, 2023)

Williams Ian: *The Fire of the Dragon*: China's New Cold War (Birlinn 2022)

Wilson, E. O. (quoted in Syed, Matthew: 2022 above)

World Economic Forum (WEF): *Global Population Ageing: Peril or Promise* (2012)

WEF: The Global Human Capital Report (2017)

WEF: Global Social Mobility Report: Equality, Opportunity and a New Economic Imperative (January 2020)

WEF: Global Social Mobility Index (2020): Why Economies Benefit from Fixing Inequality (January 2020)

WEF: Future of Jobs Report (October 20, 2020)

WEF: The Global Risks Report 2023 (January 2023)

World Inequality Report (2022)

Yeomans J & Harter F: *China "Owns the earth"*: Sunday Times (May 1, 2022)

Zuboff Shoshana; *Age of Surveillance Capitalism* (2019)

3   The Forces for Change in Education Today

"The last century was won by muscle, while this one will be won with wisdom... Last century we won by caring about myself, this century we win by caring about others." (Jack Ma, the retired head of Alibaba: Jan 6 2020)

Introduction

In the face of the immense and unstoppable forces for changing the World at large outlined in Chapter 2, the case for a fundamental, paradigm shift in education seems overwhelming and long overdue. The OECD (2022) has therefore identified five forces, in particular, that education today needs to address urgently.

Firstly Growth

The current model of unlimited growth is environmentally unsustainable and grossly unequal with the emergence of an elite few owning unimaginable wealth and with 10% of the world's population still living in extreme poverty; a world that is ageing rapidly as a third of children born today are predicted to enjoy a 100 Year Life and the percentage of those aged 80 years and over in OECD countries is predicted to double from 5% in 2020 to 10% by 2060 generating immense pressures on current health and social care systems but equally creating huge new areas of employment and market opportunity. "There is no Planet B" rather an existential need to rethink our current models of economic growth to "reconcile shared prosperity and sustainable life".

Secondly Living and Working

Identifying the skill sets needed for future learning, employability and well-being in a world of prosperity and sustainability or environmental collapse and digital servitude. In a world where 65–85% of jobs of the future are yet to be created, where non-standard work and ways of working disrupt and destroy traditional career pathways and prosperities,

DOI: 10.4324/9781003358770-4

where regular career changes and the acquisition of new skill-sets may be essential to cope with the rapid transformations of future work and job-roles; where data and intellectual property are the new sources of wealth and where digital technology (DT) is not only transforming future life but tracking and even controlling it to the point that even love and human relationships are quantified and transformed into products driven by algorithms; where family life is increasingly provisional as divorce and cohabitation rise and friends are the new family; where ageing populations are shrinking the current workforces, putting immense pressures on the traditional care services but equally creating new markets for retirement wealth within an emerging Longevity economy. Where the search for a better balance in the relationship between work and family, life seems to be driving the quality of life, while life itself seems to be increasingly quantified in an apparently insatiable search for personal perfection.

Thirdly Knowledge and Power

Big Tech is generating such an abundance of information that it is increasingly overwhelming and understood only by powerful algorithms and AI systems outside of normal legal and social controls within new virtual or fake realities outside normal ethical boundaries. Conspiracy theories thrive, trust in traditional authorities declines and democratic values and respect for the rule of law are undermined. The "wisdom of the crowds", the comfort and certainty of like-minded communities, trolls and extreme *woke cultures* are threatening to stifle free speech and open, rigorous and rational debate. Artificial intelligence promises much but without strict legal and ethical regulation, it threatens to create artificial control of human thought, privacy and decision making.

Fourthly Identity and Belonging

Where personal and social identity is no longer determined by such traditional forces as gender, family, society, nationhood or religion but by personal creation on virtual and even multiple profiles on Internet websites influenced and informed by current fads, fashions and followings in virtual communities of like-minded individuals shattering traditional bonds and loyalties and generating social fragmentation and polarisation in the process leaving the individual increasingly vulnerable, alienated and isolated amid ever-increasing concerns about young peoples' mental health and well-being. Even socialising is increasingly more virtual than physical; and while such traditional sources of collective identity as religion and trade unions are still strong in many OECD countries, the role and size of the post-war nation-state is a source of heated debate as reflected in the UK's Brexit Referendum and in today's political debates in America. International and illegal migration has become a major political issue across the OECD in terms of numbers and integration.

Finally Our Changing Nature

As both human beings and members of Planet Earth in a world increasingly driven by new technology and threatened by global warming and climate collapse as horrendous hurricanes, seismic storms and devastating bushfires become increasingly intense and regular events wiping out whole communities and destroying traditional livelihoods. Industrialisation and the carbon emissions of fossil fuels have led the UN to predict planetary collapse if the Earth warms a further 1.5 degrees beyond 2050. Human ecological footprint exceeded the Earth's biocapacity in 1970 and in 2021 we exceeded it by 70%. Meanwhile, biodiversity is being threatened with extinction by human activity with 25% of all plant and animal species now under threat despite growing attempts to create conservation areas and to green our cities. Ironically, humans are not only consuming more food but are also consuming unhealthy processed and fast food encouraged by a voracious food industry and generating dramatic rises in obesity and related ill-health in many developed countries. Human longevity is still rising but more slowly as the sciences of ageing and anti-ageing grow and some futurologists predict the possibility of everlasting life with some Big Tech figures all too eager to invest in it. Meanwhile, explorations in cyberspace grow with both virtual and augmented reality as the target of future Apple and Metaverse development.

In the face of such apparently overwhelming global issues, how does any education system possibly prepare young people for such fundamental and existential questions and their future life as individuals and families, workers and citizens on a planet and in a world that seems to be in a state of perpetual crisis and where the disunity and self-interest of the major political powers seems so immense and intense? How does education prepare and progress young people into the new economies—the green economy, the longevity economy and even the space economy Elon Musk and other acolytes are advocating? What are the skill-sets needed for future employability and human well-being in a world—or worlds—of prosperity and sustainability, environmental collapse and digital servitude? Education itself needs a post-war transformation, a paradigm shift of such proportions that it would lift it from the educational conveyor belt many writers describe today to the *social saviour* many believe is so desperately needed for tomorrow. That is the debate currently swirling around all countries post-Covid-19; that is the debate that is being driven by the UN, OECD and all the world's leading authorities and consultancies; that is the debate about a shift from 20th-century knowledge to 21st-century skills outlined in the following section.

The Case for Change

'The Economic & Employers' Case

In stark contrast to the "tortoise-like" pace of change in the education sector, employers and employees seem to be "haring ahead" in developing lifelong learning skills. According to the Carringtoncrisp/ Linkedin (July 2021) survey in July 2021, 87% of employers plan to develop a formal lifelong learning strategy and 74% already recognise or soon will recognise qualifications gained online either on their own or as complements to traditional qualifications such as degrees. Degrees and vocational qualifications remain the main employment credentials but many aspire now to Masters degrees and MBAs alongside online courses and accreditation. Employees are increasingly open to such new providers as FutureLearn, Coursera and ServiceSkills.com in providing more flexible lifelong learning (LLL) that can be "topped up" at regular intervals at low cost. Flexibility and personalisation will be at the heart of future learning; brand will be key for future providers while collaboration will become the new normal whether between employers and learning and skills providers or between traditional and non-traditional institutions. Back in 2020, the CBI proposed a world-class adult education system in the UK: a "Learning for Life" transformation.

The Educational Response

Within the world of education, the concept of 21st-century Core Skills (21CS) has taken centre stage; a concept that can be dated back to the launch of the OECD's PISA programme in 2008 (OECD/CERI: May 2008) and the publication in 2018 of results that revealed that in "only five OECD countries do more than two-thirds of young people reach or surpass PISA level 3 in reading literacy" (Canada, Finland, Ireland, Korea and New Zealand) The "one-size fits all model no longer meets the needs of a knowledge society". Schools today need to be reinvented rather than simply reformed. They are entrenched in a such a highly bureaucratic model with vested interests and centuries-old habits, that it is almost impossible to overturn. They restrict and constrain learning rather than nurturing and promoting it and today's assessment and accountability regimes are likely "to stifle the very approaches to learning and innovation" that reforms seek in principle to encourage and bring in. There needs to be a "strategic shift from school learning to lifelong learning". As Andreas Schleicher, Director of Learning at the OECD (Foreword to OECD 2030 Project: 2018) elaborated "education success is no longer about reproducing content knowledge, but about extrapolating from what we know and applying that knowledge to novel situations" (or even to what we don't yet know).

Education today is much more about ways of thinking which involve creative and critical approaches to problem solving and decision making. It is also about ways of working, including communication and collaboration, as well as the tools they require, such as the capacity to recognise and exploit the potential of new technologies, or indeed, to avert their risks. And last, but not least, education is about the capacity to live in a multi-faceted world as an active and engaged citizen. On the basis of that philosophy, the OECD proposed a Learning Framework for 2030 based on the Vision that "every learner develop as a whole person, fulfil his or her potential and help shape a shared future built on the well-being of individuals, communities and the planet"; a philosophy in which *Learner Agency* is the key and a resilient *Student Growth Mind-Set* is essential in enabling young people to navigate the complex and uncertain world ahead supported by co-agency; by the support and guidance of teachers, school managers, parents, employers and communities. Students will need to be able to navigate through uncertainty across a wide variety of contexts and to engage with the natural world, its fragility, complexity and value. "Disadvantage is not (always) destiny" and even disadvantaged students can succeed "where there is a Growth Mindset of resolute ambition amongst students and a positive school climate where students feel wanted and worthwhile".

On that basis, the OECD (2020) predicted four possible scenarios for education by 2030:

- Schooling Extended whereby the current roles, structures and methodologies of school systems today continue with some shift towards more personalised learning.
- Education Outsourced in which diversity and diversification of types of school, types of learning and certification driven by increasing parental choice become the dominant features.
- Schools as Learning Hubs in which schools retain a central role but more as a community hub co-ordinating and commissioning learning across a variety of local organisations and partnerships.
- Learn-As-You-Go in which public education is dismantled in favour of a "free market" in education based on Digital Technology and AI as learners become "prosumers" and teachers producers of future learning.

The World Economic Forum (WEF) has also sought to define New Models of Education for the Fourth Industrial Revolution. Its 2020 Report set out its Education 4.0 Framework and proposed three skill-sets for 21st century learning: problem-solving; collaboration and adaptability arguing that "The transition to Education 4.0 will also require learning mechanisms that more closely mirror the future of work and that take full advantage of the opportunities offered by new learning technologies" It will need learning ecosystems that are personalised and self-paced, accessible and inclusive, problem-based and collaborative; lifelong and student-driven. As Google for Education has explained (2022) "The idea that you educate for jobs is an idea of the past. Today you learn to create your future, to create your job". Education 4.0 requires a global mind-shift from education as a one-off age-based phase (5–25) to education as a lifelong career and lifestyle experience; "a mindset that is ready to learn, unlearn and relearn beyond the scope of formal education" through say a 60-year curriculum. The new imperative for education is to help develop the skills needed for machines and humans to work together and to develop workplace skills that are not easily automated. This will require time and space in the school timetable and greater collaboration between education and employers. "Careers education is no longer about steps to a perceived future but learning to navigate a pathway through an ever-changing job and opportunity universe". Vocational education should be elevated alongside or even above academic qualifications and schools should consider adopting such education-work partnerships as the Meister School scheme in South Korea whereby schools align themselves with particular industrial sectors such as media, banking and telecoms. As the Education 2050: A Glimpse at the Future (February 2022) report illustrates, the future of education and learning is no longer the paradigm of the past but a strategic shift to the online world of the future with the EdTech industry and now Big Tech offering a whole new world of educational possibilities ranging from the Khan Academy to Elon Musk's Ad Astra and Ad Nova schools. As has been happening in the world of work, home-learning for part or all of the school week becomes increasingly possible allowing us "to create education that is tailored to the individual, universal in nature, and decentralized in structure" enabling every student "to find their own path to success, learning and assessed at their own level not by age or grade". This debate and the comparable contributions from UNESCO and the World Bank have helped put Future Education firmly on the international agenda with an increasing focus on the following.

Twentieth Century Skills and Competences (21CS)

Needed for learning and living in the century ahead; the skills and capabilities identified originally by the US Army War College in tackling VUCA (volatile, uncertain, complex and ambiguous) situations. Think tanks such as the Partnership for Education's Framework for 21st-century learning and the WEF have sought to distil such skills down to a manageable number with the 4Cs of Creativity, Critical Thinking, Communication and Collaboration emerging in several models as "the highest-level transversal skills or meta-competencies-that allow individuals to remain competent and to develop their potential in a rapidly changing professional world" alongside adaptability, resilience and problem-solving (Branden Thornhill-Miller et al: March 2023). In terms of progress to date, however, while the 2020 Worldwide Educating for the Future Index (WEFFI) put Finland, Sweden and NZ in the top three, the UK has fallen from 10th to 15th (Catherine Lough: *TES Magazine* (Jan 2020)).

The Curriculum Framework

Best suited to 21st-century learning; the debate now emerging in the UK after Rishi Sunak's intervention as to whether the Baccalaureate Framework used across Europe might better serve future learning in England too, in providing the breadth and balance for personalising school education, in integrating learning and assessment and in providing clearly staged progression pathways through and into the world of ever-changing work.

The Pedagogy of Learning

The teaching methodology needed for the radical shift from teacher-centred to student-centred learning, from a focus on knowledge and content to skills and capabilities, leadership and teamwork and learning from real-life situations. Personalised and tailor-made instruction will be needed to help ensure that all learners reach their full potential and students will need to be better prepared to interact with their own communities, virtually and in person, and to deal confidently with people from different cultures, while continuing to learn throughout their lives. Teachers will remain, but their roles will be extended as mentors, mediators and guides, facilitators, learning coordinators, assessors, and designers and compilers of learning tools; testing will most likely continue but assessment will become more individualised and formative. Self-responsibility for learning will be essential and learners can expect to determine what their learning profile will look like and which learning styles work best; teaching and learning styles such as those described in the Open University Innovating Pedagogy Report (2022); techniques such as dual learning combining classroom theory and industrial application as in apprenticeships; hybrid models such as blended learning combining online and face-to-face learning; influencer-led education via such social media as YouTube and Tik-Tok and micro-credentials where educational agencies including the OU offer a vast range of MOOCs or massive open online and accredited short courses for both professional and personal e-portfolios.

Educational Assessment

An area seen by many as the key to liberating 21st-century learning from conformity and compliance to a narrow academic curriculum but equally the area most likely to generate resistance and opposition. A traditional curriculum built around subjects based on knowledge and content is relatively easy to teach and assess within the confines of a classroom or examination centre with pen and paper answers marked and moderated by outside examiners and external exam boards. Assessing skills and competences such as the 21CS listed above, in real-life scenarios, is far more challenging and as Ester Care and her colleagues (2018) have discovered quite rare in practice. While 21CS are increasingly prominent in many countries' national documentation, "many countries are still using 20th-century teaching methods and assessments to teach them" and worse relying on pen and paper tests as proxies for real-life capabilities. 21CS require a paradigm shift in assessment as well as one in curriculum and pedagogy; a paradigm shift that requires expertise in defining such skills, designing authentic forms of assessment, identifying criteria to prove their mastery and creating Learning Pathways that genuinely represent the higher orders of such skills. Such definitions need to allow for significant cultural differences as well as those created by a given occupational sector or social situation. Western societies, for example, have very different ways of communicating or working than many Asian cultures; different professions or work environments have different communication systems and standards; different social situations require different ways of interacting. As the NESET II review of Assessment Practices for 21st-century learning (2021) concluded, at present "there is no single method that would fully measure key competences and transversal skills, nor serve as best practice for student assessment" although the OECD is leading on developing them. Moreover, according to Branden Thornhill-Miller and his colleagues (2023), there are now a number of international educational ranking systems to help to promote best practice and high performance such as the IICD's (International Institute for Competency Development) 21st-century Competencies Assessment Framework for Institutions. The real challenge though is not just assessing individual 21CS skills and competences but assessing groups of them in combination in real life. Problem-solving and performance at the highest level require all four 21CS. Effective collaboration, for example, requires clear communication based on critical examination and creative innovation. These authors are therefore now working on a "Crea-Critical-Collabication" model of dynamic interaction of the 4Cs with VR technologies increasingly providing the means to create learning and practice environments and AI the means to assess and profile individual performance and progress. Alternatively, perhaps as Valerie J Shute suggested back in 2009, 21CS are better assessed by stealth, by building assessment into the activities being tested as in "serious games" competitions rather than as traditionally as an add-on and separate exercise; a marriage of gaming and assessment that many young people might welcome. Certainly, as the Pearson's Review about the Future of Qualifications and Assessment for 14–19-year-olds in June 2021 found, young people continue to value formal qualifications as documented accreditation of their years of learning but only if such qualifications are objectively and fairly assessed and have real currency with end-users. Students in this survey argued too, for more continuous, formative assessment using new technology and they identified four guiding principles that they believed should underpin future learning, namely, that education should be *empowering*; curriculum, qualifications, assessment and teaching should be *coherent* but *adaptable*; and *innovation* should inform and enhance 14–19 education and "unleash the power of technology".

Education and New Technology (EdTech)

Certainly. the real game-changer for education and learning in the 21st century looks to be the adoption and adaptation of new technology; an adoption by education that so far has proved painfully slow compared to most other sectors but one accelerated by the Covid-19 lockdown and mass transfer to the likes of Zoom, MS Teams and Google Classroom. Smart Learning Environments are already well established in FE and HE combining formal and informal learning and formative as well as summative assessment in "tracking both student behaviour and their performance to inform future guidance and if necessary intervention to prevent premature drop-out or withdrawal" (Cheung SKS et al: 2021). The ultimate goal though, according to the OECD (2021), is a fully integrated learning eco-system in which AI technologies talk to each other, inform all stakeholders of student progress and propose solutions to improve student performance, motivation and morale; and in the process free up 13 hours a week of teacher-time for preparation, administration, evaluation and feedback to direct student support and learning so making teaching a much more attractive and satisfying profession (McKinsey & Co: Jan 2020). The Luwan No. 1 Central Primary School in Shanghai China, for example, has a digital students' app providing a detailed, holistic portrait of each and every student while its digital teaching system provides teachers with teaching aids that include data on lesson preparation, classroom orchestration, intelligent assessment and intelligent home-work review alongside an intelligent tutoring system that supports students directly in accessing resources, tools, pathways and personalised guidance. This model is now used by more than 250 schools across China while Tongji University in China is now a test centre demonstrating the *digital classroom* of the future (OECD: 2023).

Educational Robots

Are now starting to appear in school classrooms. Robot Elias is now a popular visitor to schools in Tampere in Finland while Bee-Bot, Dash, Root, Edison, BAO and Ozobot entertain pupils across the globe. According to Rosie Sage (2020), humanoid robots such as Pepper and NAO are established classroom assistants and their visual and intuitive interface makes the content creation process easier, allowing customised teaching activities on a one-to-one basis or in small groups. They can introduce new topics and help students with project-based learning, problem solving and analytical skills, motivating students and encouraging creative and innovative thinking. They can even empathise with students, help develop their self-confidence, interpersonal, social and emotional skills and work effectively and patiently with students with SEN, autism and emotional and behavioural disorders. Shy and withdrawn students will often open up to humanoid robots rather than to adult humans. Most especially, social robots can befriend younger students and so introduce them—and adults—to the idea of robots as partners, even friends, in the future world rather than aliens about to take us over. Italy is currently engaged in testing out the potential format and framework for a "robot-led curriculum and learning pedagogy" for all sectors of education while in the UK, the Robotics Challenge is now an annual STEM-based competition led by Engineering UK. According to Dev Saransh Sood of Softbank Robotics (November 13, 2020), there are already over 13,000 humanoid robots working in colleges and universities across the world. However, while the potential for robot teaching assistants in the classroom is immense, so too are the potential risks; risks that include breaches of privacy, malfunction, robot dependency and pupil withdrawal from adult guidance; a potential form of psychological imprisonment or robot control as robots learn more and faster than fellow pupils or teachers. Teachers will soon need training on robot use in the classroom to ensure control, safety and accountability as well as how to plan lessons assisted by a robot. So, while robots are likely to become a feature of virtually all areas of contemporary life, and accepted as such, so the need to plan for and regulate this emerging invasion of traditional human life is urgent rather than allow it to emerge haphazardly or worse through corporate gain rather than public benefit. The ultimate challenge for the robotics industry, though, is how to develop "common-sense" in humanoids.

Common sense may be an innate ability in humans but it is not one that simple mass data analysis will unlock on its own. Similarly, while AI works perfectly well in a strict rule-bound world, the human world is full of contradictions, rule-breaking behaviour and chaos that at present confounds software engineers. As does the notion of fun; a major motivator for learning for children but as yet one apparently outside humanoid understanding.

Nevertheless, the **Ed-Tech Market** is expanding at pace and predicted to rise to $300 billion by 2024, and according to PWC (2023), it is set to boost the global economy by £1.4 trillion by 2030 led by companies such as Adobe systems, Apollo Education Group, Blackboard Inc, Cisco Systems, FUTURELEARN, Google, Khan Academy, Pearson, MS and Udemy. "It is clear that AR and VR have the power to revolutionise learning by making the learning experience more immersive and engaging. It transforms learners from passive spectators into active explorers". It is already widely used in medical training and new employee induction, simulating customer experiences with people through apps such as Snapchat. EdTech is at the heart of the Fourth Industrial Revolution and the UK is a Edtech pioneer with British start-ups attracting 41% of all European investment in 2019 according to Tech Nations Data Commons. World-wide, the leading companies include Nuance (speech-recognition/translation); Knewton (adaptive learning technology for HE, tracking and programming learning at different levels) and Century Tech's personalised learning plans and teaching resources.

However, as described earlier, the concerns and critiques of New Technology and especially of Generative AI have also grown exponentially. As Dirk van Damme of the OECD has warned (February 4, 2021) AI may soon prove to be "the deepest and most disruptive change in the 21st century" with quantum computing the next new powerhouse of the Internet. The threat of AI on future jobs is now well documented; the dangers for education are not; not least because "what students need to learn at school will progressively be informed by what makes humans truly human"; skills that include ethical decision making, empathy, ingenuity and inter-personal relationships from loyalty to love. While "the most experienced and capable students will learn a lot from sophisticated, AI-supported educational resources, the more vulnerable, struggling students will not succeed if they have to miss the human factor of a real teacher". Hence the need for AI strategies and the sort of strict codes of conduct being developed in Australia, Canada, Japan, the UK, EU and the USA and in the OECD's (2019) Principles on Artificial Intelligence. In November 2023 the UK hosted a global summit on AI and is proposing to set up an AI Safety Institute charged with identifying and quantifying AI risks. However, as Ilkka Tuomi explained back in 2020, AIEd developers are already fast becoming an elite breed and AI is in danger of increasingly becoming the brain-child of a few high-tech companies with Super-Tech powers such as America, China and India potentially determining the future of humankind. As John R. Allen of the Brookings Institute (January 31, 2019) has prophetically forewarned. "these technology developments are on the cusp of ushering in a true revolution in human affairs at an increasingly fast pace ... and the winners of this upcoming AI-defined era in human history will be the countries and companies that can create the most powerful algorithms, assemble the most talent, collect the most data, and marshal the most computing power". This is potentially a "hyperwar" that could leave nations across the world dependent on and subservient to one or more AI superpowers, certainly if China has its way. "AI/EdTech promises to usher in a bold new era of human history, one where the machines we create will often at times be smarter, faster and more powerful than those who created them. The ethical issues involved are immense and what the country needs is a *comprehensive strategy* for reimagining our education system at the national level."; a warning and a recommendation that governments across the world are now increasingly taking seriously and one that UNESCO, in particular, is constantly reiterating. The UNESCO (2023) Global Education Monitoring Report, for example, calls for much stricter governance and regulation of EdTech and its development, greater teacher engagement in designing and implementing new tech, in owning and controlling its transformation and in being continually upskilled to deliver it, supported by a continuous programme of research into best practice under a strict risk management regime to identify and monitor emerging and future risks to support prevention as well as cure; exactly the sort of strategy the UK is now proposing to develop. As Luan Hui et al (2020) have argued "few data scientists and AI developers are familiar with advancements in education psychology" so it is imperative that educators lead technology, not technology lead education, that teachers become more skilled and knowledgeable about AI and that governments provide a more suitable legislative framework to protect personal data from unscrupulous collection and commercial exploitation; an alliance and dialogue between *cold technology and warm humanity* in a paradigm shift in future and lifelong learning that supports both teachers in teaching and learners in learning. The advent of "strong AI", of Generative AI, is already leading the paradigm leap required for the smarter, personalised learning of the future as it advances beyond simply classifying and analysing mass data to imitating such human cognitive abilities as making generalisations drawn from prior experience, proposing new solutions and mimicking human speech and scripts. As Andreas Schleicher of the OECD has commented while Covid-19 opened schools and universities to Big Tech and converted apps such as Google Classroom and Google Meet into the patron saints of remote learning and education, it equally opened up the classroom to new technology but left in its wake an escalating digital divide between advantaged and disadvantaged households and the absolute need according to Audrey Watters (2022) to make sure that schools are "about what the public wants and not what Edtech companies want them to look like".

So, in one form or another, restrained or unleashed, educational technology will have a major part to play in the future for education in the 21st century. Some even see it as *THE* future of education in the 21st century. Certainly, AI is here to stay and while AI-powered chatboxes like ChatGPT and virtual assistants will provide students with personalised feedback and support and Big Data Analytics will provide teachers with data and insights into students' learning needs; VR technology will effectively provide differentiated and personalised learning experiences for students and "the Metaverse, a virtual space, will allow students to experience things that may have been impossible in the real world". Technology is breaking down geographical barriers and making education more accessible to students in remote and under-privileged areas across the world. And to support and encourage EdTech adoption by education, the World Bank/GEEAP has created a Global Education Evidence Advisory Panel to advise on educationally "smart buys" for 2023 particularly for developing nations; a sort of *Which Guide* to Future Education and Technology to sit alongside comparison sites like EdTech and EdSurge.

The Digital Generation

And behind this great technological leap into the digital unknown lie the Digital Natives: Generation Z, Alpha and Beta. They have grown up with new technology and see it as an integral, even normal part of daily life. As the 2023 Opinium survey found, no previous generation has experienced such rapid and unprecedented change on so many fronts as today's Gen Z and Alpha". "Yet they are ambitious, socially conscious and driven, with a clear vision of what they expect from the education system". Namely, a *holistic experience* with an increasing focus on such real-life skills as personal finance, politics and wellbeing; and particularly on new technology and digital/virtual learning, areas where teachers often struggle. Success for them, according to this multi-national survey, is not determined by professional achievement alone but by personal fulfilment in having a job that they love, one in which they can help others as in the pandemic and one that enables them to make a difference in the world; in industries such as health, computing/ technology, creative industries, government/uniformed services, education/teaching, sports and leisure, engineering and mechanics, animal care, law alongside such non-traditional subjects as video-gaming, AI, robotics, cryptocurrency and advance mathematics. However, traditional classrooms are often seen as distracting and lessons boring, while 69% of the students involved really enjoy using technology to learn and communicate and feel that they learn best through play. Pupils do not see EdTech replacing teachers but supporting them as robots or avatars in personalising learning. "The nature of learning is changing and schools & teachers need to change with it".

The new generation of AI-assisted technology may also allow for the assessment of competences that were previously hard to assess and introduce such new forms of assessment as games-based and simulation-based methodologies as in the Digital Campus being developed in China. Digital Technology (DT) may therefore help improve equity by increasing and simplifying learning access especially for students with disabilities or special needs be they visual impairment, hearing disorders or ADHD; identify students falling behind, disengaged or at risk of dropping out, personalise learning to fit the student rather than fit the student to the pace and level of learning in the classroom and extend learning into the home through intelligent tutoring systems. However, as this report also revealed apart from Korea, Singapore and China, "the majority of students have limited digital navigation skills", most schools still seem ill-equipped to realise the full potential of Digital Technology and "most OECD countries do not have clear regulatory requirements ... as of 2023".

Teachers and EdTech

Clearly, the advent of EdTech will equally require a technological revolution and skills upgrade among teachers who are often technologically behind their students. The OECD report on Teaching for the Future (2023) has gone so far as to suggest that rather than Digital Technology threatening the teaching profession, it may actually save it by releasing teachers from many of the mundane and administrative tasks that often overwhelm their workloads and so allow teachers to reassert their professional status and so, according to the 2019 European Forum on the Future of Learning, convert:

- Teachers from 20th century "content conveyors" into 21st century "content curators", to create new content in new forms and enable learners to investigate, critique and engage with knowledge rather than simply absorb and memorise it. 21CS will therefore become crucial to 21st century learning.
- Teachers into being creators and co-designers of EdTech not just its customers and users, championing and prioritising ethical issues and

learner safety/ privacy; partners in the shift into the 'deeper learning' implied by Generative AI.

In turn, smart technology such as social robots can directly help classroom management, the learning and assessment of individual pupils, their performance and their teachers; and so help elevate the teaching profession world-wide to the high social status enjoyed in such leading educational nations as Finland and Singapore. Teacher Training, in turn, needs to be more classroom based than theoretical and alternative routes into teaching need to be expanded as Teach First in the UK and Teach All globally have sought to do. Teaching and learning need to be owned and developed by the teaching profession itself rather than directed from on-high recognising as the OECD declared in its 2023 report "The heart of great teaching is not technology, it is ownership". As experience in the Netherlands and elsewhere has shown when teachers assume ownership of their profession, professional standards rise, and professional pride and reputation set new standards of expectation and performance. Government-driven educational reforms, in contrast, tend to be slow, bureaucratic and resisted. The 21st century and its students do not have time for that sort of long-term change; change that may well change direction at the next election and leave classroom teachers isolated at the bottom of a decision-making chain that they have no part in creating yet are held accountable for delivering. The future world of learning can no longer be static and bureaucratic. It has to be dynamic and deliver change at speed, not as isolated individuals but as a collaborative profession driving improvement and experimenting with innovation with "professional norms of control replacing bureaucratic ones so in turn encouraging teachers to trust students learning more and encourage the critical and creative thinking skills that are central to success in the 21st century". As the HertsCam Network proclaims teachers need to become agents of change rather than simply deliverers of a proscribed curriculum. Education authorities, in turn, need to take a lead on supporting innovation and in disseminating the benefits through digital resource centres that schools and colleges can borrow from free of cost so encouraging EdTech testbeds and pilot programmes in a safe and controlled way incentivised by public funding. Wales and Ireland have been cited as examples of best practice with the Welsh Government's Hwb EdTech programme hailed as "world class" by MS, Google and Adobe while Ireland's Digital Learning Framework (DLF) seeks to outline what *effective and highly effective practice* in the use of digital technologies actually looks like and support schools and teachers in delivering and developing it. Denmark's universal log-in system, dubbed the Netflix model, helps to store data in one safe site and the Estonian

Education Information System (EHIS) is a state database that coordinates and secures all educational data about education institutions, students, teachers, teaching materials within a common "data-lake". The shift to professional autonomy and the encouragement of innovation in schools in an age of innovation is vital if education is the serve society and its economy effectively and unleash learners true skills and potential. That needs government leadership and support but it also needs the education sector to come out of isolation and engage business at large and EdTech in particular rather than sit back in fear that it will take it over and turn it into yet another profit-making enterprise. The challenge is how to create a relationship, even a partnership with EdTech ensures that the needs of education over-rule the needs of profit. Such a shift in learning, ownership and design may have radical implications for redesigning the rest of the traditional education structure from the shape and role of the school day and year right through to the school timetable, staffing model and classroom design. It might equally offer the opportunity to change significantly the role and engagement of parents as learning support and assessors. The adoption and integration of EdTech requires a whole school approach and a strategy with strong and effective school leadership, clear roles and responsibilities for all staff and proper funding alignment. As the 2019 European Forum report concluded while EdTech has the potential to transform English education, EdTech on its own "has little intrinsic value without an underpinning strategy for realising educational outcomes". Hence the need for government to balance the inevitable tensions between commercial and public interests, ensuring that Big Tech's engagement in education is not solely for profit but a partnership governed by an appropriate level of regulation and control; ensuring that digital developments are inclusive and help bridge or even mitigate the current educational digital divide; ensuring that there is a clear National Strategy and Leadership and that educational institutions adopt a whole school/whole system approach not just tag EdTech onto existing and dated pedagogies. It will need to build Digital Leadership, win over the hearts and minds of teachers as well as upskilling them; and win over parents and all stakeholders in the need, value and the model of learning transformation that digitalisation offers with opportunities for teachers to test and experiment within a safe and controlled space in the US EdTech Genome Project.

The Classroom and the School of the Future

Such a radical shift in the traditional paradigm of education inevitably raises significant questions not only about the future of all and any national education *system* but also the future of such traditional educational institutions as the School, the College, the University and even the Classroom. A.Gocen and colleagues foresee the Classroom of the Future (2020) as one of learning zones that "equipped with technological equipment, provides new teaching methods by age, is created according to a flexible learning design, and has teachers as guide and students as active and productive individuals". The debate about the future of the School as an institution has been even more fast and furious with organisations such as the International Commission on the Futures of Education (March 2021) ardently arguing that while CV-19 brought home the potential for remote learning, it equally taught us the importance of the school, of structured and collective learning and "the intense difficulties of transferring education into the home". As Covid forcefully reminded us, "family and economic life is regulated by the pace of school" one that starts in early childhood but that now extends throughout life. Moreover, the school is one of the few institutions that can still protect the poorest and most vulnerable. It is not just a centre of learning but potentially a centre for social services, a forum for collective learning that "cannot be fully replaced by distance or remote learning" and a safe environment for children to take risks and experiment with possibilities. "Self-education is important, but it is not enough. What we know depends, in large part, on what others know ... Human beings learn but human beings are also capable of being taught- this beautiful dynamic, which connects us to one another" and inter-generationally, to the past and the future. Schools need to operate in an educational ecosystems not in isolation and education needs to be regenerative with traditional skills joined by 21st-century skills, empathy and emotional intelligence combined with cognitive intelligence, knowledge being treated as "work in progress", a human heritage and an intergenerational conversation. Pedagogy, however, must change and must help shift learning from teacher-delivered content to student-driven enquiry working in collaboration not in isolation, working for common action and benefit not just competing for individual benefit and promotion (see also the work of Valerie Hannon and her colleagues programme for identifying The Future School: 2021–23).

The Future of Higher Education

The future of higher education and even that most hallowed institution, the University, is equally now in question. While Rahul Choudaha and Edwin van Rest (January 2018) believe HE has the opportunity to grow exponentially with the arrival of mega-cities and the shift to lifelong learning already evident in high-income countries, the 2020 KPMG report on higher education is less optimistic. The post-war "golden age" for universities, argues this report, is now coming to an end as a result of the declining value and attractiveness financially and personally of a degree qualification. Escalating tuition fees are leaving graduates with lifelong debt and increasingly excluding students from poorer households. The escalating costs of HE provision are leaving universities with a declining capacity for reducing costs while employers are increasingly disillusioned with the products of a traditional university education. Graduates seem to lack the skills and attitudes needed for working in 21st century work environments yet many of them seem to see themselves as entitled to expect automatic promotion and top salaries while others are having to accept jobs "below" the level of their perceived qualifications. The traditional university model of education no longer fits the needs of the Fourth Industrial Revolution, and the new EdTech alternatives look more attractive, personal, flexible and effective. "Universities will always have their place" but in the Age of the Customer "they will become the minority". The gloss has come off, the digital revolution is generating a wave of more cost-effective online educational alternatives, while China and the emerging nations are developing their own HE systems rather than sending students abroad to the West. In the Age of the Consumer, the Student Experience is paramount but post-covid that experience has been distinctly poorer. "The next shift will likely be from mass face-to-face to mass digital learning" as learning starts to flip with courses increasingly delivered through technology and supplemented by face-to-face support rather than the other way round. The University Campus will become a minority experience; the augmented experience combining physical and virtual learning more of a reality for more and more students alongside possibly occupational experience for those combining work and learning.

To regenerate the HE market, KPMG suggests a far more flexible and fluid business model for HE in the 21st century, one that is based on:

- Borderless boundaries, competing globally as well as locally.
- Shorter courses and degrees via micro-credentials, nano and curated-degrees and hybrid blends thereof particularly as the proportion of students who are "digital-natives" grows and new models of digital learning and assessment evolve.
- Experiential Learning; learning by doing and on-the-job accreditation is likely to grow especially with employer sponsorship and engagement in course construction.
- Life Long Learning as the need and demand for retraining and job transition accelerates and becomes a social and economic essential across the lifetime of today's students.
- A shift within Education sector to a Platform model whereby HE commissions, quality assures, accredits and franchises local or international providers.
- Lifestyle Integration whereby higher education through shorter, part-time and digital courses will become an integral part of future students

lifestyles as they "learn & earn" in tandem rather than through a full-time 3–4 year education.

Utkash Amitabh (2020), in turn, predicts a "great unbundling" of traditional degree courses with increasing focus on 21CS, shorter return-on-investment (ROI) courses to support career choices and a switch to lifelong learning with personal support operating alongside AI. A shift in learning to match the shift in longevity involving a portfolio of qualifications to support a portfolio of careers with funding systems like Income Share Agreements (ISA) becoming more common. The MOOC (massive open online course) movement with its own certification and nanodegrees represents the first wave of this "unbundling" to be followed soon by new modes of networking, the shift to soft skills and the emergence of organisations where membership, association or affiliation signals equal or greater competence. Such disruptive innovation may put 50% of all colleges out of business. The future of learning, he believes, lies with AI + Community Colleges because AI alone is too distant and impersonal to sustain learning.

So what next? Research into the Future Teacher and the Future Student?

Educational Best Practice: Rankings and Reviews

In 2008, the OECD launched the Programme for International Student Assessment or PISA system to test the critical thinking of 15-year-olds across the OECD in maths, science and reading. The aim is to test students' real-world problem-solving skills and knowledge and on that basis begin to compare the quality of national education systems internationally and so promote a global debate about best practice on the understanding that a high-quality education system is usually correlated with economic success. Over 85 countries involving some 6,300 students currently take part and in the 2018 PISA, China, Singapore and Estonia topped the PISA chart with the UK 10th after Ireland and just before Slovenia with the US 22nd. The 2022 rankings were similar despite an overall fall across the OECD in subject scores as a result of Covid. Significantly, in both 2018 and 2022, the level of life satisfaction amongst UK students was well below the OECD average." The 2018 tests also revealed that "over ten million students represented by PISA in 2018 were not able to complete even the most basic reading tasks and often these were 15-year-olds in many of the wealthier countries of the OECD, countries where a student's socio-economic background *still seems to be the key variable in academic outcome*". "Moreover, there has also been no real overall improvement in the learning outcomes of students in OECD countries, even though expenditure on schooling rose by more than 15% over the past decade alone". In contrast, the four provinces selected to represent China "outperformed their peers in all of the other participating education systems" despite the level of income in these four provinces being well below the OECD average while "among OECD countries, Estonia has advanced steadily to the top, despite the fact that expenditure per student remains about 30% lower than the OECD average". As the 2018 PISA report continued, "In a world shaped by artificial intelligence, education is no longer just about teaching people something, but about helping people build a reliable compass and the navigation tools to find their own way through an increasingly volatile, uncertain and ambiguous world" yet in the age of smartphones and fake news "fewer than 1 in 10 students in OECD countries was able to distinguish between fact and opinion". School choice is often critical yet in many countries social diversity is low and "a typical disadvantaged student has only a one-in-eight chance of attending the same school as high achievers". In the OECD's view, it is clear that students in the 21st century need very positive "growth-mindsets"; the belief that they can improve themselves and not just leave it to fate or "fear of failure". East Asia is an example of a growth-mindset instructional system where mastery not just memory is required by all students; a philosophy that needs consistency across all teachers and reinforcement by parents. In Finland special needs, teachers work with classroom teachers to identify and support pupils needing extra help and alternative learning styles alongside its "pupil's multi-professional care group" that meets at least twice a month; a form of educational levelling-up rather than the levelling-down often generated by the traditional streaming systems used in many mainstream schools. Future economic success depends on all students succeeding not just the academically able. Otherwise, a substantial minority leave school feeling failures; a feeling that is likely to promote depression, alienation and dissatisfaction for the rest of their lives. It's not a simple binary choice of competitive or co-operative environments but a balance whereby competition is enjoyed by all but where competition does not define or determine any one student. The OECD has also developed a PISA for Schools Report 2022; a PISA-based test for schools (PBTS) to use themselves that measures not only 15-year-old students' knowledge but "how well students can extrapolate from what they know and apply their knowledge creatively in novel contexts". The PBTS is intended to provide school-level results for school improvement and benchmarking purposes.

As intended, the advent of the OECD's PISA tests has generated an intense international educational debate ever since with OECD nations jockeying for top positions. It has inspired a profound soul-search amongst the nations of the OECD about best practice and a global search for the "magic formula" that might unleash the talents of all children—and adults—not just the abler academically and in so doing help transform future economic performance and social harmony. The

McKinsey reports on education in five continents (2007 onwards) was one of the widest and deepest of searches for the world's best-performing schools but it too reflected just how elusive that educational "magic dust" is in practice. Funding alone apparently is not the answer, nor class size, structural change or even *Building Schools for the Future* programmes. Rather, as this study of 25 of the world's school systems, concluded, it is a mixture of ingredients; a mixture that, "irrespective of culture", needs to put three ingredients first, namely: Getting the right people to become teachers; secondly developing them into effective instructors and thirdly putting into place systems and targeted support to ensure that every child is able to benefit from excellent instruction. In other words, build the system around excellent teachers—not, as often happens, the other way round—and set high standards and expectations for students and teachers with appropriate funding, governance and support. "The quality of a school system rests (ultimately) on the quality of its teachers" and "reform efforts which fail to address these three drivers are unlikely to deliver the improvements in outcomes that system leaders are striving to achieve".

Teaching, therefore, needs to be a highly attractive and esteemed profession; entry to teacher training both selective and effective and starting salaries competitive not excessive". The top-performing school systems tend to recruit teachers from the top third of their cohort graduates (or higher as in Korea and Finland) but also encourage entry from alternate sources or later in life. They equally operate quite rigorous selection procedures to screen out unsuitable candidates which is why some of the top school systems select candidates *before* they start their teacher-training courses not afterwards as in most education systems. In this way, only the ablest or most motivated get through and entry to teaching, like medicine, is therefore seen as highly competitive so avoiding an over-supply as in most school systems. Teaching in Singapore and Finland, for example, is a highly desirable career not a second or third choice and places on Teacher Training courses are deliberately limited. "In all of the systems we studied, the ability of a school system to attract the right people into teaching is closely linked to the status of the profession".

Similarly, "the only way to improve outcomes is to improve instruction". As Tony Blair would say "Professional development, professional development, professional development" with individual teachers fully aware of their weaknesses and their pathway to self-improvement and best practice based on "high expectations, a shared sense of purpose, a collective belief in their common ability to make a difference to the children they serve". System change alone is not enough. "Structural reform has no discernible effect unless it changes what goes on in the classroom for *each and every student*." But getting the right people to become teachers-and stay teachers- and developing them into effective instructors is only the first step. High-performing school systems go beyond this and "put into place processes which are designed to ensure that every child is able to benefit from this increased capacity" and expertise. High-performing systems not only monitor school performance but also intervene at the level of the individual student, developing processes and structures within schools that are able to identify whenever a student is starting to fall behind, and then intervening to improve the child's performance. The system needs to ensure that every child, rather than just some children, has access to excellent instruction to the point that "the best systems have produced approaches to ensure that the school can compensate for the disadvantages resulting from a student's home environment". Standards are high but external curricula prescription is low in countries such as Finland where teachers are trusted and treated as professionals and so are given the freedom to innovate and explore. While external intervention for failing or under-performing schools has its place, "the best systems take these processes inside schools, constantly evaluating student performance and constructing interventions to assist individual students in order to prevent them falling behind". Finally, while focusing on the quality of the teaching profession and on pupil experience in the classroom is key, no school system has successfully improved without talented school leadership, highly effective governance, equitable funding for all schools and a high-quality curriculum offer in a virtuous *Learning Circle* that engages parents and employers as well as students and staff. Educational reform based on structural reform alone simply disrupts and destabilises teaching and learning without affecting the root causes of under-achievement. The top-performing school systems go deeper and seek to improve "the quality of instruction of a single teacher and then develop the systems to create these conditions for all teachers" and from that improve instruction for all students.

However, as the McKinsey study of *How the world's most improved school systems keep getting better* (2010) illustrated, maintaining improvement is often as hard as achieving it in the first place. School leaders in such schools need to have a voracious appetite for relentless improvement; an improvement plan based on clear identification of the improvements needed and the creation of an effective improvement plan that reflects the history, culture and politics of the national system. Such a plan needs to know and understand the key factors in both sustaining any improvement achieved and in "igniting" the next take-off from poor to fair; fair to good; good to great and great to excellent with a proportionate decline in external control and guidelines as schools become more confident and collaborative, self-motivated and achievement hungry with mediating support from the centre and from cross-school partnerships. In citing examples from Chile, Latvia and Hong Kong, the report concluded that the starting or take-off point for sustained school improvement is usually one of three things: a political or economic crisis; a critical national report or the energy and input of a new political leader or government. Of the three, "the injection of new leadership appears to be by far the most important factor" but this depends on their tenure of office, level of authority and ability to sustain support for improvement amongst key stakeholders from government and governors through to employers, parents and teaching unions. Such long-term drive and commitment stands in stark contrast to the decision-making process in the UK where a British Prime Minister may be in office for five, even ten years but few education ministers last more than two. The Roadmap in this McKinsey series is a valuable example of a system improvement framework and possibly a benchmark for evaluating education in the UK and England.

National Reviews

As the PISA results indicate, certain nations or regions seem to have created educational systems within which students not only perform consistently well against the PISA benchmarks but also display high levels of independent learning and personal resilience—or what the OECD now calls *growth mindset*. Below are examples taken from two very different parts of the world; Finland (and Estonia) from the Scandinavian and Nordic School of high-performing countries; Singapore as an outstanding example from South-East Asia.

Finland

According to the OECD Education Policy Outlook (2022) and OECD Country Note 2018, Finland has starred as a top-performing nation in PISA ranking since its inception although performance recently in maths, reading and science has declined amongst the lowest-achieving students. Socio-economic background has a low impact on educational performance in Finland and Finnish schools focus heavily on equity and on preventing low achievement although the gender gap in reading is one of the widest across all participating OECD countries. Attainment rates in upper secondary and tertiary education are higher than OECD average with one of the highest enrolment rates in Vocational Education & Training (VET), one of the lowest school drop-out rates in Europe apart from that amongst young migrants; and one of the highest scores in the Survey of Adult Skills. In total, 67% of Finnish students recorded a "growth mindset" in 2018 though less so for boys and disadvantaged students. Teachers are trusted professionals, competitively selected and required to have a master's degree that includes research and practice-based studies. They are relatively well-paid, and as highly valued as doctors and lawyers. Schools have average autonomy over the curriculum and assessment compared to other OECD countries but below-average autonomy over resource allocation. There are no national standardised tests or high-stakes evaluations. The Finnish Education system is a partnership between central and local authorities with government setting educational priorities and municipalities overseeing school delivery and providing school support services, funding and personnel.

A four-year National Education & Research Development Plan outlines education policy priorities so aiding continuity outside the usual electoral cycles and Finnish expenditure on education as a percentage of GDP is "one of the highest shares of public funding among OECD countries". The Finnish system is razor-focused on equity and quality, on reducing inequities such as gender and migration and on strengthening school leadership, teacher CPD and developing persona-lised and life-long learning supported by new technology but without standardised tests, heavy homework, HE tuition fees or private schools. The unswerving aim is to develop the individual potential of each and every child under the mantra "We can't afford to waste a brain". Vocational learning is high skill and revered without any social stigma, pupils are given significant autonomy and trust and schools are considered equal—if not elite—so there's no need to "school-shop" as in the UK. Teachers assess pupil progress and the Ministry of Education tracks overall progress through national sampling rather than by school league tables and inspections as in the UK. Accountability is not required when teachers are so highly selected and trained and co-operation not competition is the hallmark of the Finnish system with pupil welfare and happiness a priority; a priority reflected in a shorter school day, a later start to school life at age 7 and a shorter stay of only 9 years within compulsory education followed by a wide choice of tertiary options. Teachers often remain with their tutees for up to 6 years, mentoring as well as teaching them and so strengthening mutual trust, continuity and maturity. Learning is seen as a holistic experience to be enjoyed not feared. Public confidence in Finnish education is high with all parents aspiring to a great educational opportunity for their children.

These reforms began some 50 years ago and have been part of a new post-war social contract and a national dialogue with the trade unions, employers, public and educationalists. The move to a comprehensive education system began with the Basic Education Act in 1968, a new core curriculum in 2004 and a holistic approach to child learning that reflected both Finland's shift to a more egalitarian society and its economic shift from manufacturing and agriculture to the new communications technologies. There is a recognition, however, that with Covid and the shift to the Fourth Industrial Revolution of automation, AI and robotics, a rise in youth unemployment is likely to require further adaptations to its education system, notably in the development and delivery of transversal 21st-century skills and competencies. Finland's Right to Learn Programme (OECD Report No 61) is Finland's answer to its recent decline in international assessment and to the emerging gaps in performance particularly amongst disadvantaged and immigrant groups. As Barbara Bruins has argued (Oct 2015), underlying the "magic" of the Finnish education system lies three highly motivating forces. Firstly teachers do not have job security as civil servants as they are employed by individual schools and so can be relatively easily dismissed. Secondly, school budgets depend on enrolments and so schools must strive for excellence to survive. Thirdly, students face challenging performance pressures not so much in compulsory school but in the examinations for entry to Finland's highly competitive tertiary institutions. So, as in Estonia, accountability is built into the Finnish system for all its actors, even if they don't actually have a word for it.

While Finland has been an educational "superstar" since PISA began, **Estonia** has emerged quite recently at the top of PISA charts. Estonia is a tiny country of some 1.3 million people; a relatively poor agrarian society that emerged from the collapse of the Soviet Union but one that then transformed itself through a *Digital Leap* into the unknown with the wholesale adoption of e'technology. Estonia characterises itself as a *start-up* nation with 99% of government services delivered online, pupils learning robotics from age 7 and all schools hard-wired using electronic timetables and soon online marking and exams so dramatically reducing staff workloads. It is a relatively "classless" society and its education system is fairly decentralised between the state which sets out national policy and overall strategy and the municipalities which oversee the school system. According to the OECD Better Policies for Better Lives Series: No 47 (2020), "the Estonian education system is considered one of the best-performing systems among OECD countries, combining quality and equity in education. As a testament to Estonia's commitment to education excellence and continuous improvement, the design of the Estonian Education Strategy (EES) 2035 goes beyond strict education performance and encompasses the knowledge, skills and attitudes for people to thrive in the 21st century".

The Estonian system, however, is not without its faults and the Estonian Ministry of Education & Research is reviewing its education monitoring system, seeking to select the indicators underpinning the EES 2035 that will identify disparities between schools and regions, gaps between formal and informal learning and between different types and levels of education. In particular, the aim is to bring external evaluation into closer alignment with school self-evaluation, improve stakeholder's such as students and parents understanding and capability in data management and engage teachers and institutions in using such data learning so that they feel real ownership of and value in collecting it and do not therefore dismiss it as irrelevant to their school or a threat to them. Estonia now has an EC/OECD grant for developing an Education Monitoring System (EMS) or Data Road Map to underpin and inform its 2035 Strategy; one that is SMART, informs practical action and may offer a guide or model for countries such as the UK, particularly, the smaller nations such as Scotland, Wales and possibly Northern Ireland.

Singapore in SE Asia

Singapore has been described by the Institute for the Future of Education (2020) as a "gentle nation" with no resources except its people and one where parental engagement in education is exceptional. Teachers are an educational and social elite selected from the top 30% of each cohort and the government puts great trust in their professional expertise. Education is in very close alignment with Singapore's economic ambitions and it's belief that Life Long Learning is the key to future life; a belief backed up by a Skills Future Credit of $500 to support ongoing learning throughout adult life. Class sizes are high at 40 but that allows government to pay teachers well.

Singapore is a city–state that has leapt from a country of low literacy into a top PISA performer since its independence from Malaysia in 1965 through an intense and highly competitive education system. The Ministry of Education (MoE) has traditionally exercised tight central control of the curriculum, the examination system, teaching methods and schools within a culture of teaching and testing through high-stakes terminal exams. However, under the Educational Mantra *Thinking Schools, Learning Nation*, Singapore is making a step-change in strategy towards a more relaxed educational environment where teachers and schools have greater autonomy and decision-making power, the curriculum is slimmed down, the volume of testing reduced and the status of applied and vocational education upgraded. This is all part of a shift towards *Skills for the Future* that include creativity, new technology and the *Child of the Future*, one who is self-confident, self-directed, independent, critical, creative and a good communicator; a self-directed learner, an active contributor who is a team worker, innovative and effective capable of taking the initiative, taking calculated risks and who strives for excellence but who is equally a concerned and responsible citizen rooted in Singapore with a strong sense of civic responsibility.

Eight changes have been introduced into Singapore's education system in recent years to moderate Singapore's very intense exam

system during the period 2019–2024 including the withdrawal of
exams and weighted assessments from certain primary levels, extending the Direct Admission Scheme (DAS) to secondary education
and introducing a healthy lifestyle programme in all primary and
secondary schools. There is an increased use of aptitude tests for entry
to tertiary institutions not just exam results and a new technical
diploma is to be introduced; an apprenticeship based in collaboration
with employers. In addition, the PSLE scoring system used for
secondary school entry is to be modified to include informal assessment tests such as class tests and group projects; grading is to be
withdrawn from the Holistic Development Profile or Report Card
(HDP); a new criterion-based grading system introduced for foundation level subjects and more incentives for performance in higher
Chinese language exams. The 2018 Talis Survey showed very
high levels of teacher and school leader job satisfaction, self-esteem
and professional development although school leader and teacher
attrition and the levels of stress through too much administration,
marking or responsibility for results were higher than OECD average.
Teacher autonomy in the classroom is high and encourages innovation and professional collaboration within and between schools. As
Mike Thurman General Secretary of Singapore Teacher's Union
explained in his interview with the Institute (April 2020) Singapore
does not have many resources; "Our people are our only resource" so
we must nurture them. "Parents take huge responsibility and ownership over students' education, especially in the early years". There are
no quick fixes. Teachers are key and we only recruit from the top
30% of the cohort with 8–10 applicants for every teaching position.
Education is now clearly aligned with the economy and commonly
recognised as such so creating a clear consensus around educational
objectives and outcomes, curriculum design and 21CS and helping
to mobilise education-employer-parental partnerships and support.
Overwhelmingly though "teacher ownership, teacher leadership and
teacher autonomy are very critical". As with doctors we trust their
judgement and professionalism so professional development is a
crucial investment. "We have this simple saying in Singapore: the
principals take care of the teachers; the teachers take care of
the students". The child is at the centre of everything but now the
notion of lifelong learning is also being embedded at every level of
society. We no longer talk about employment; we talk about *employability*. Hence the Singapore Government's focus on continual
retraining funded by the Skills Future Credit of 500 dollars to every
Singaporean over 25 years as a means to creating graduates that are
self-confident, active contributors, constant citizens and self-
directed learners. As Singapore's new education minister Chan

Chun Sing declared in 2022 (*Strait Times,* February 2022) as the world economy shifts, so must Singapore. Pre-defined pathways to success are no longer guaranteed. Rather employment is constantly changing and so must education and training both at school and throughout life. The time from education and training to market must be shortened if Singapore is to remain competitive.

Singapore is but one example of the educational superstars pouring out of East Asia. Korea, Taiwan and Shanghai could equally be cited but undoubtedly China is now the world's educational superstar not only because according to UNESCO (2021), it has the most extensive education system in the world with 282 million students, 17.32 million teachers and over 530,000 schools but because it currently has one of the top PISA performers. China is a classic long-term planner with an Education Modernisation Plan for 2035 with a focus on AI in education and vocational education and training, with "Socialism with Chinese Characteristics" incorporated into the curriculum and with pupils needing to be "well-rounded". Private tutoring companies and private schools were banned in 2022 possibly as part of a shift towards total state control of education but equally to halt the competitive ethos and resulting inequalities emerging from this experiment in using market forces in education.

India, too, has global ambitions according to the Brookings Report in October 2020 and India's EdTech industry is expected to reach $30 billion in the next ten years led by start-ups such as BYJU, Teachmint, QUIZZIZ, Unacedemy and Ingenuim education. And behind the Asian educational tigers lie the sleeping lions of Africa, a continent teeming with youthful talent but lacking at present the infrastructure and expertise to effectively teach and assess 21CS nor the political stability to undertake long-term change. This explosion in educational ambition and drive for excellence in the developing world contrasts starkly with the relative stagnation evidenced by such advanced nations as Great Britain and even the USA. America may still be a superpower but its education system was described as 'requiring improvement' to use Ofsted terminology in the Institute of Educational Sciences Report on the Condition of Education in 2022 despite the billions of dollars spent on it; failures that include inadequate state and local government funding; a serious decline in school safety with a series of high profile mass shootings and a failure to integrate new technology into teaching and learning and education management. Standardised testing has led to a culture of "teaching to the test" and the US lags mid-table in the 2018 PISA results despite the 2002 federal commitment to No Child Left Behind.

Commentary

So what are the lessons to be learnt from such international reviews by the UK? Both the Dept of Education's own report on "effective school improvement" by Greatbatch & Tate in July 2019, and the 2021 EPI study concluded that "there is no single approach that is causally linked to better outcomes. Instead, high-performing countries employ a multitude of varied approaches". Like the McKinsey series cited earlier, what such studies have shown is that substantial and sustained educational transformation tends to need three critical features or drivers:

Firstly, a crisis or challenge that sparks national debate on the need for fundamental change.

Secondly consensus-building and clarity about who is involved and at what level.

Thirdly, a political system and tenure of office of key decision makers in maintaining momentum and direction of reform. Decoupling education reform in England from the electoral cycle and having it under its own renewal tenure would significantly overcome the huge system disruption that is often characteristic of English policy-making.

Finally, while the OECD's PISA programme has been spectacularly successful in generating international debate about educational standards and performance over the last twenty years, it is not without its critics. Jerry Gao (April 2022) has accused the OECD PISA framework of both a First World, western cultural bias in the questions set and topics chosen and the potential unfairness of allowing participant countries to "cherry-pick" the students that they submit. In Gao's view, far from PISA being a fair and objective international educational comparison, it has become "politicised" and manipulated by certain countries as part of an international "bragging rights" campaign. Steve Hodge (2021) goes further, arguing that the 21CS and Lifelong learning in the Education 4.0 paradigm developed by international agencies such as the WEF and OECD is based on a particular model of future work—Industry 4.0—despite their explicit acknowledgement that the future of work is increasingly unforeseeable. Moreover, the knowledge, skills, attitudes, values and competencies proposed in say the OECD Learning Compass 2030 or UNESCO's global paradigm are not new but revised versions of taxonomies dating back to the 1950s. Montse Gomendio; Spain's ex-Minister of Education and previously Deputy Director for Education at the OECD goes further and in a scathing critique of PISA's Mission Failure (2023) argues that "after almost two decades of testing, student outcomes have not improved overall in OECD nations or most participating countries" despite the adverse publicity, the international reporting and resultant "shocks" to many national educational systems. In her view, "policy recommendations cannot be universal, because what works in egalitarian societies may lead to bad outcomes in societies with high levels of inequity". Rather change should be sequential and context-dependent on the political and social tensions in a particular country; not one-size-fits-all. As Svein Sjorberg (2019) has commented, the PISA initiative has certainly helped elevate education high up the global agenda. It has excited an interest and determination for improving life and learning for both young people and now for all age groups with publications such as "Baby-PISA" for early-years education through to the PBTS for schools and PIAAC for Adult Skills. However, it is equally in danger of generating a *PISA Syndrome*; a highly competitive market environment that reduces the purpose of education to what can be measured on a single dimension, in a single test, on a single day, on a single sample of 15 year-old students so ignoring all its other less quantifiable but ultimately critical responsibilities such as socialisation, motivation and progression. PISA has become a political project used and often abused by governments to justify educational reforms that are at odds with the educational community in an era when educational reform has become "a policy epidemic" (Levin B: 1998). PISA has promoted national "soul-searching" but as yet, to produce substantial overall improvement.

Bibliography

Allen John: Brookings Blueprint for the Future of AI series (January 31, 2019)

Amitabh Utkash: How Technology Will Transform Learning in the COVID-19 Era: Network Capital (August 31, 2020)

Auld E & Morris P: The OECD and IELS: Redefining early childhood education for the 21st century: *Policy Futures in Education*, 17(1): 11–26 (2019)

Big Innovation Centre (with APPG & KPMG): Learning to Learn: the Future-proof Skill (2019)

Brookings Institute Report on India: Sahni, U: India's National Educational Policy 2020: A reformist step forward (2020).

Bruins Barbara: Education for Global Development (October 2015)

Carringtoncrisp/Linkedin: The Future of Lifelong and Executive Education (July 2021)

Cheung SKS et al: Shaping the future learning environments with smart elements: challenges and opportunities: *International Journal of Educational Technology in Higher Education*, 18: 16 (2021)

Choudaha Rahul & van Rest Edwin: Eight Megatrends shaping the future of global higher education and international student mobility: *Megatrends2030: Studyportals* (January 2018)

Dept of Education: Opportunity for All: Strong Schools with Great Teachers for Your Child (March 2022)

Education: Education Reform in Finland and the Comprehensive School System (September 2, 2019)

Education Policy Institute (EPI) Mills Bobbie: How Leading Educational Nations Develop and Reform Their Curriculum Systems (January 2021)

EDUCAUSE Horizon Report: Teaching and Learning Edition (2023)

Ester Care et al: *Education System Alignment for 21st Century Skills: Focus on Assessment*: Brookings (November 2018)

European Forum on the Future of Learning (2019)

Fishman T & Sledge L: *Reimagining Higher Education (in US): How Colleges, Universities, Businesses, and Governments can Prepare for a New Age of Lifelong Learning*: Deloitte Consulting (May 2014)

Gao Jerry: *The Flaws in How We Compare Education Systems*: DataDrivenInvestor (April 19, 2022)

Global Partnership for Education: 21st Century Skills: A Landscape Review (January 2020)

Gocen Ahmet et al: Teacher perceptions of a 21st century classroom: International JNL of Contemporary Educational Research, 7(1): 85–98 (June 2020)

Gomendio Montse: PISA mission failure: *Education Next*, 23(2): (2023)

Google for Education: The Future of Education: Trend Forecast Report (2022)

Google for Education: Education 2050: A Glimpse at the Future (February 4, 2022)

GoStudent: Future of Education Report (2023)

Greatbatch D & Tate S: UK Dept of Education report on "effective school improvement activity in five countries with high-performing-school systems" (July 2019)

Hannon Valerie: The Future School: UCL Centre for Educational Leadership (January 2023)

Hannon V. with Temperley J: *Future School*: Routledge (2022)

Hannon V and Peterson A: *Thrive: The Purpose of School in a Changing World*: CUP (2021)

HM Government: National AI Strategy (September 2021)

Hodge Steven et al: Who is competent to shape lifelong education's future? Internat. *JNL of Lifelong Education*, 40(3): 193–197 (2021)

Hui Luan et al: Challenges and Future Directions of Big Data and Artificial Intelligence in Education: *Frontier Psychology* (October 1, 2019)

Institute for the Future of Education: Observatory IFE: Singapore's Educational Success Story (April 10, 2020)

International Commission on Financing Global Education Opportunity: Investing in Education for a Changing World (2016)

International Commission on the Futures of Education Report: Education in a post-Covid world: Nine Ideas for Public Action (March 2021)

Institute of Educational Sciences: Report on the Condition of Education (2022)

JISC: The Future of Assessment: Five Principles, Five Targets for 2025 (Spring 2020)

JISC: Elevating the UK Further Education and Skills Sectors (October 2020)

JISC: AI in tertiary education (April 2021)

KPMG International: The Future of Higher Education in a Disruptive World (2020)

Levin B. An Epidemic of Education Policy: *Comparative Education*, 34(2): 131 (1998)

Lough Catherine: *21CS: Global best & Worst at 21st Century Skills*: TES Magazine (January 2020)

Ma Jack: The retired head of Alibaba: IQ, EQ and LQ: WEF (January 6, 2020)

McKinsey & Company: Five Continents Series: How the world's best performing school systems come out on top (2007); How to improve student outcomes (2017); How the world's most improved school systems keep getting better (2010); Drivers of Student Performance: Insights from Europe (2017), from Asia (2017), from Latin America (2017), from North America (2017), from Middle East and North Africa

McKinsey & Co: How Artificial Intelligence Will Impact K-12 Teachers: Bryant J. et al (January 14, 2020).

NESET II: Assessment Practices for 21st-century Learning: Review of Evidence (2021)

Newton DP & Newton LD: Humanoid Robots as Teachers and a Proposed Code of Practice: front. *Educ* (November 5, 2019)

No 14: Cynthia Luna Scott: The Futures of Learning 2: What Kind of Learning for the 21st Century? (November 2015)

No 15: C.L. Scott: The Futures of Learning 3: What Kind of Pedagogies for the 21st century (December 2015)

OECD Education Policy Outlook (2022) and OECD Country Note 2018: Finland

OECD: Finland's Right to Learn Programme; Achieving equity and quality in education (Report No 61): (September 2022)

OECD Country Note on Results from 2018 PISA: (Estonia)

OECD: Enhancing Data Informed Strategic Governance in Education in Estonia: Education Policy Perspectives (2021)

OECD Better Policies for Better Lives Series: Education Policy Perspectives No 47 on Estonia (June 2020)

OECD: Pushing the Frontiers with Artificial Intelligence, Blockchain and Robots (2021)

OECD Education and Skills Today: Artificial Intelligence and What It Means for Education Tomorrow (February 2021)

OECD: Work on Education & Skills: Policy Products & Services for Countries (2021)

OECD:PISA for Schools Report 2022: a PISA-based Test for schools (PBTS)

OECD: PISA for Schools: How The European Schools Compare Internationally (2022)

OECD: Teaching for the Future: Global Engagement, Sustainability and Digital Skills: International Summit on the Teaching Profession: (2023)

OECD's PISA programme in 2008 (The OECD/CERI: 21st Century Learning: Research, Innovation and Policy: May 2008)

OECD: Schleicher Andreas, Director of Learning at the OECD (Foreword to OECD 2030 Project: The Future of Education and Skills: Education 2030 (2018)

OECD: PISA 2022 Results: Vol. 1 The State of Learning and Equity in Education: Vol. 2: Learning During-and from-Disruption (2023)

OECD: PISA 2018: Insights and Interpretations (2019)

OECD: Back to the Future of Education: Four OECD Scenarios for Schooling (2020)

OECD: *Mansilla V. B. & Schleicher A: Big Picture Thinking*: OECD (2022)

OECD: Preparing Our Youth for an Inclusive and Sustainable World: The OECD PISA Global Competence Framework: Ramos G & Schleicher A (2015)

OECD: Education Policy Outlook: Shaping Responsive and Resilient Education in a Changing World (2021)

OECD: Better Life Index: Education (2019)

OECD: AI Principles Overview (May 2019)

OECD: *Trends Shaping Education 2022*: OECD Library (2022)

OECD: Principles on AI (2019)

OECD: Van Damme Dirk: Education and Skills Today (February 4, 2021)

OECD Observer: The secret to Finnish education: Trust: Schleicher Andreas (January 2020)

Open University Report (Innovating Pedagogy Report 2022: Open University Innovation Report 10)

Opinium: Future of Education Report 2023 survey of Children (Generations Z & Alpha) and Parents/Guardian's views of Education in the Future in 6 European countries (Austria, Germany, France, Spain, Italy & UK)

Parsons Kathyn: *ChatGPT Has Entered the Classroom-and Teachers Are Woefully Unprepared*: Sunday Times (May 7, 2023)

Partnership for Education: Framework for 21st Century Learning (January 2016)

Pearson: The Future of Qualifications and Assessment for 14-19 year olds (June 2021)

Pearson: Qualified to succeed: Building a 14–19 Education System of Choice, Diversity and Opportunity (March 2022)

PwC: Educational Technology Market Report (2023)

Sage Rosie: Education for Robotics: (June 27, 2020)

Sahni Urvashi: *India's National Education Policy 2020: A reformist step forward*: Brookings Institute (October 2, 2020)

Shute Valerie et al: *Melding the Power of Serious games and Embedded assessment to Monitor and Foster Learning: Flow and Grow*: Routledge (2009)

Sjoberg Svein: The PISA-syndrome-How the OECD has hijacked the way we perceive pupils, schools and education: Confero, 7(1): 12–65 (2019)

Sood Dev Saransh: Softbank Robotics (Classrooms of the Future blog: November 13, 2020)

Strait Times Report on Sunday Times Education Forum speech by Chan Chun Sing, Singapore's Education Minister (February 10, 2022)

Tech Nations Data Commons (2019)

Thornhill-Miller Branden et al: Creativity, Critical Thinking, Communication, and Collaboration: Assessment, Certification, and the Promotion of 21st Century Skills for the Future of Work and Education: Journal of Intelligence 11(3):54 (March 15, 2023)

Tuomi Ilkka: *The Impact of Artificial Intelligence on Learning, Teaching and Education: Policies for the Future*: eds. Cabrera M et al: Publications Office of the EU (2018)

UNESCO/Unicef: China Case Study (2021)

UNESCO: Education 2030: AI and Education: Guidance for Policy Makers: Miao F. et al (2021)

UNESCO: *Reimagining our Future Together: A new social contract for education*: International Commission on the Futures of Education (2021)

UNESCO: Education Research and Foresight Working Papers.

UNESCO: Global Education Monitoring Report (2023)

Vegas E & Winthorp R: *Global Education: How to Transform School Systems?* Brookings Institute (November 17, 2020)

Vivekanandan Ramya: *Integrating 21st century Skills Into Education Systems: From Rhetoric to Reality*: Brookings Institute (February 14, 2019)

Watters Audrey: Blog "We need schools to be more about what the public wants and not what EdTech companies want them to look like." (March 2022)

Whiting Kate: *These are the top 10 job skills of tomorrow-and how long it takes to learn them*: WEF (October 21 2020)

Williams Matthew S: Life in 2050: A Glimpse at Education in the Future: Innovation (June 8, 2021)

World Bank/GEEAP: Global Education Evidence Advisory Panel to advise on educationally "smart buys" for 2023

World Bank Group: Realizing the Future of Learning: From Learning Poverty to Learning for Everyone, Everywhere (December 2020)

World Economic Forum (WEF): Schools of the Future: Defining New Models of Education for the Fourth Industrial Revolution (January 2010)

WEF (in collaboration with the Boston Consulting Group): New Vision for Education: Unlocking the Potential of Technology (2015)

WEF: Education, Skills and Learning:10 Reasons why Finland's education system is the best in the world (September 10, 2018)

WEF: From Wall-less Design to Robotics Training: Meet the 16 Schools Defining the Future of Education: Salyer K (January 14, 2020)

WEF: 4 trends that will shape the future of higher education (February 7, 2022)

WEF: Catalysing Education 4.0 (May 16, 2022)

World Population Review:Education Rankings by Country 2023 with USA, UK & Germany top three.

4   A Framework and Strategy for Educational Change

"As we face a very uncertain future, the answer is not to do something better than what we've done before. We have to do something different. The challenge is not to fix this system but to change it; not to reform it but to transform it."
Robinson K & Aronica L (2016)

Introduction

So, if, according to Chapter 1, the English education system is no longer fit for "future" purpose in the mega-force world of the 21st century described in Chapter 2, how might the forces for change in Chapter 3 be mobilised in bringing English education back to the forefront of world education and truly serve each and every child and adult in preparing for the century ahead? Rishi Sunak's proposal in September 2023 for a British Baccalaureate certainly enlivened the educational conversation in England and possibly helped promote ideas for quite radical change. But what is really needed is a full-scale transformational plan and a strategy for implementing and embedding it not only within schools and colleges but within life in the 21st century itself. *Learning for Life* will need to become an essential feature of everyone's life in a century of global turbulence and uncertainty with the 2008 Financial Crash of 2008, Covid-19 and now Climate Change, Ukraine and Gaza are just a taste of the "eruption & disruption" ahead. We clearly need a new National Conversation about Education in England. We need a new National Educational Mission, a new Education Mantra, an *Education, Education, Education* Part II with the imagination, ambition and funding to follow. We need a new theory of education, a new science of learning to inspire and inform future practice if judgements in teaching and learning are to be informed by educational need not political expediency or electioneering. We need a revolution in education not from the top down but from the ground up particularly as it is the countries that have turned away from the "standards" movement dominant in countries

DOI: 10.4324/9781003358770-5

like the UK, that are now leading the way on the PISA league tables; countries such as Estonia, Singapore and Finland building on trust: trust in teachers; trust in schools; trust especially in students—all students—and their increasing ability with new technology to learn, as lifelong learners, for themselves.

Educational Transformation Across the UK

In contrast, to England's often disjointed and piece-meal approach to educational change, Scotland and Wales have both embarked on more long-term transformation programmes; even if they are still very much "works in progress". **Scotland's Curriculum for Excellence (CfE)**, for example, was described by the OECD in June 2021 as "an inspiring and widely supported philosophy of education. Its framework allows for effective curricular practices and for the possibility of a truly fulfilling education for learners ... education is a source of pride in Scotland, which shows in the broad commitment to CfE and educational excellence for all. It has been granted great importance in the political debate to a degree that would be the envy of many a system". However, as the rest of this OECD report explains putting great educational ideas into everyday practice is a challenge in itself and at present, Scotland's educational system is described as "a busy system at risk of policy and institutional overload" with the OECD follow-up report in October 2021 strongly recommending a radical rethinking of the assessment system for older pupils and the need to move away from terminal exams alone towards a combination of continuous assessment, school-based exams, teacher assessment and external exams. As the Stobart Review in 2021 concluded the "national examinations (in Scotland) have often inhibited changes to teaching and learning" with the examination syllabus becoming the de facto curriculum and teachers teaching to the test; a diet of central examinations at 16, even when few students now leave education at that age. That is "something no longer seen in most other assessment systems". Professor Stobart therefore recommended a major overhaul of Scotland's examination system to come in line with the ambitions of the CfE and the world ahead and to serve and support *all* learners not just the academically able. The Muir Report (March 2022) went further and recommended a substantial devolution and redistribution of power, influence and resource within the Scottish Education system down to local authorities, schools and teachers alongside greater trust and collaboration amongst all stakeholders with more targeted support and resource on early years, learners with additional needs and teacher CPD. The whole examination and assessment system, in its view, needs a fundamental review and realignment with the agreed purposes of education, parity of esteem between academic and vocational education and qualifications and a radical reduction in bureaucracy and educational paperwork. In particular, Muir advocated a renewed National Conversation on the future of Scottish education, a refreshed vision for the CfE, a new Qualifications body and a National Agency for curriculum development, accreditation and assessment, learning, teaching and leadership, the creation of a new independent inspectorate and the combining of the Care Inspectorate and HMIE inspections for Early Years establishments. The Withers Report (June 2023) was equally scathing, highlighting in particular, "a lack of strategic leadership and effective governance". "We don't have a whole-system view" or a clear set of priorities at either national or regional levels so the problem is confusion rather than complexity with funding and qualification pathways too fragmented and prescriptive based on a multitude of criteria and performance outcomes. Given "the complexity of pathways, the lack of understanding of the jobs and occupations of the future and the proliferation of agencies and actors, it is perhaps no great surprise that not all individuals are able to make smart or informed choices about their future careers". There is a clear need for "substantive, structural reform of the delivery landscape including a clarification-and in some cases rationalisation-of the remits and roles of national bodies" particularly the division between skills for the economy and education for the learner. Most especially, the simplistic division into academic and vocational pathways is a false and hugely damaging dichotomy that has no presence in reality but culturally persists even in the way the Scottish Funding Agency (SFA) is structured and operates. "We cannot continue to present these as two diametrically opposed and competing ideologies". It "exacerbates tensions, harms the journey towards parity of esteem and, at worst, stigmatises certain destinations for further learning and employment" and the students following them. As James Withers fervently warned unless appropriately managed the endemic academic-vocational divide could easily re-emerge in the future. "Without change to the shape of the current agency landscape, even with the right policy intent and clearer leadership, the system is likely to continue to be challenged by the same issues it currently faces". Hence his recommendation that education and skills come under one ministry. As Priestly and Shapira (2023) summed it up, these reports "paint a stark picture of curriculum reform that has diverged considerably from its original aims with significant unintended consequences for young people, teachers and schools, and serious equity concerns".

Wales

The Welsh journey to educational transformation began much later than Scotland's, with an OECD report in 2014/2015 on Improving Schools in

Wales and the Donaldson Review in 2015. The 2014 OECD report heavily criticised the Welsh education system highlighting low pupil performance, unsatisfactory assessment and evaluation arrangements, patchy primary-secondary transition and a weak PSHE offer. In the OECD's view, the education system operating in Wales in 2014 was one within which there is "a high degree of prescription and detail in the national curriculum, allied to increasingly powerful accountability mechanisms (which have) tended to create a culture within which the creative role of the school has become diminished and the professional contribution of the workforce underdeveloped … .inhibiting professionalism, agility and responsiveness in dealing with emerging issues and (leading to) frequent political interventions in non-strategic matters"; with the effect, all too often, of reducing the role of primary schools to the task of "teaching literacy and numeracy and secondary schools simply to preparing for qualifications". The national curriculum of 1988 has become outdated and overtaken by such global phenomenon as the world wide web and globalisation. It has become "overloaded, complicated and in parts, outdated" and "no longer meets the needs of the children and young people of Wales. The case for fundamental change is powerful". Upon this sweeping critique, the Donaldson Review sought to set out the foundations for a New National Educational Framework based on a Curriculum defined as "including all the learning experiences and assessment activities planned in pursuit of agreed purposes of education" and founded on four Capabilities needed for all children and young people, six Areas of Learning and Experience 3–16 and the three Key Competencies of literacy, numeracy and digital competence to be delivered by all teachers within a seamless 3–16 curriculum. The transition phases would need to be removed and progression be based on *Progression Steps* with associated *Achievement Outcomes* rather than on age-based criteria as at present so allowing abler learners to progress at their own pace and slower learners to receive additional support. Wider skills such as critical thinking should be embedded within each area of learning rather than taught separately. The Welsh language should be strengthened within the curriculum and the National Assessment and Evaluation Framework be made simpler and include both teacher-led and learner self-assessment, to support learning and progression with a deliberate distinction between assessment to support learning and assessment required for accountability. In particular, the professional autonomy and creativity of teachers to design and deliver appropriate teaching and learning alongside excellent and committed leadership at all levels in the education system needed to be reaffirmed and reinforced through the principle of subsidiarity to inform and guide the engagement of schools and teachers directly in owning, designing and developing the new curriculum on the basis of national guidance and professional development. In particular accountability systems need to "make a constructive contribution to learning" and its agreed purposes and "avoid the detrimental effects of high-stakes performance measures". The Welsh Strategy was reviewed again by the OECD in 2017, and its recommendations were incorporated into the Welsh Government's 2017–2021 Action Plan: Education in Wales: Our National Mission while the draft White Paper in Oct. 2019: Fit for the Future: Education in Wales, authored by Professor Calvin Jones provided a down-to-earth critique of the challenges facing Welsh education. It declared that "GCSEs are no longer fit for purpose" and that there is a case for their replacement with "narrative-based assessment" that tells employers exactly what learners are all about. Assessment needs to be value-added and pupil centred, vocational streams to be high quality and employer-engaging while cross-disciplinary teaching is "a core requirement" and school funding needs to be increased and "hypothecated". The OECD Review in 2020 praised the clear vision at the heart of the new curriculum, its four purposes and six broad Areas of Learning and Experience and cross-cutting competencies in literacy, numeracy and digital competence; its co-constructionist strategy and the clarity of communication and the strength of its leadership of what is now recognised as a "national mission"; a national mission reflected in the significant improvement in Wales PISA scores in 2018 although "equity remains a concern". Wales has successfully mapped out its policy plan to move away from what had become a highly prescriptive national curriculum, to one that focuses on the future, is adapted to learner's diverse needs and puts the teachers and principals back into positions of leaders of learning and teaching. The policy vision is clear and looks to the long term, representing "a shift from what had become a managerial education system to one based on trust and professionalism". The new curriculum framework aspires to best practice in terms of 21st-century learning and gives high levels of agency for all stakeholders. "The challenge for Wales at this stage is to remain true to the vision while shifting the perspective of the strategy from being policy-driven to one focused on schools." The new curriculum for Wales is the cornerstone of the country's efforts to turn its education system from a performance driven education with a narrow focus, to an education system based on commonly defined learner-centred purposes "with a Vision that all children and young people achieve the four purposes of becoming ambitious and capable learners, enterprising, creative contributors, ethical, informed citizens and healthy, confident individuals who are ready to lead fulfilling lives as valued members of society" The 2021 OECD Review noted, however, that while the planned shift in evaluation and assessment arrangements—and the new inspection regime—is progressing, the lack of clarity about the future of high-stakes exams risks undermining teacher motivation for and focus on learning new assessment techniques. So, real progress has been made in Wales but major surgery on assessment still needs to be undertaken. The next challenge, as Jack Fawcett and Russell Gunson of the IPPR (2019) have argued, is to update the whole of the Wales Skills Strategy with clear guidance for "the skills system as a whole", replacing the existing school leaving age of 16 with a new *skills participation* age of 18 and so simultaneously tackling the emerging effects of automation, Brexit and an ageing population and driving forward the Lifelong Learning Revolution in Wales.

England and Regional Transformation

Scotland and Wales clearly now have immense experience in undertaking wholesale educational change; lessons that England can possibly learn from. However, as outlined in Chapter 1, the major educational reform programmes in England such as comprehensive schooling and New Labour's 14–19 reforms have been far more piece-meal and sector-specific whether that be secondary schools, HE or post-16 education and training. Moreover, beneath all these reforms, inequality and the disadvantage gap have remained stubbornly persistent and after Covid-19 even grown. Hence the post-Brexit Levelling-Up agenda adopted by the Johnson Administration (2019–2022) and recommended by such think-tanks as the Sutton Trust. Such an area-based strategy, however, also resurrected memories of previous attempts at "levelling-up" disadvantaged regions and areas of which the London Challenge was an outstanding example. According to JRF/Institute for Government report in 2014, "local authorities in inner London went from the worst performing to the best performing nationally" and the London Challenge provided "a distinct example of public service improvement that is practitioner-focused, highly collaborative and applied across a city-wide system" driven by committed professionals, a powerful sense of moral purpose and a close working relationship of officials, advisers, ministers operating with a shared, data-led view of the strengths and weaknesses in schools across the capital. However, extending this strategy in 2008 to the Black Country and Greater Manchester was, according to the Dept for Education Research Report (2010), a step too far; a strategy neither as effective nor as sustainable in the longer run. Although the proportion of schools rated good and outstanding increased as did the attainment levels of secondary pupils eligible for free school meals (FSM), as the 2023 GCSE results illustrated while London has continued to excel, Greater Manchester and the Black Country have once again fallen behind. As David Parry (2019) subsequently argued "the key to any area-based programme must be an education masterplan". London had that and has now become "a beacon for other English conurbations" not only during the Challenge programme itself (2003–2011) but in the way it was sustained under the follow-up London Leadership Strategy programme "Going for Great" (G4G) 2009 0nwards and its "Olympic-style" sense of mission and collaboration. Extending a City Challenge-type programme to the rest of England, as proposed in the 2022 White Paper, however, is likely to face immense challenges given the underlying level of disadvantage. As the Education Endowment Foundation concluded in 2021, external intervention strategies are often viewed with great suspicion and distrust at the local level until it is clear that long-term ownership and control lies with the local community and its schools. Moreover, as the EPA programme of the 1970s and 1980s amply illustrated, education cannot level-up on its own. It needs to be an integral part of an industrial and economic regeneration programme or else these areas just sink back down, particularly if the UK continues to fragment after breaking away from the EU and as the regions of England as well as the devolved nations of the UK campaign for greater autonomy, if not self-rule. Despite the apparent shift to autonomous academies and MATs, English education is still highly centralised; still strictly under the control of the DfE through the national curriculum, the national inspection regime and national funding. As the 2022 Sutton Trust: Social Mobility Report concluded "the (UK) education system as a whole has failed to function as the great social leveller". Home background and the workplace are still at least as important as education in determining mobility prospects and "in terms of absolute social mobility, the evidence suggests that a former golden age of upward mobility has been replaced by a modern era of declining opportunities and more limited upward mobility". A widening family divide, an intergenerational divide "has emerged for children growing up in the early 21st century" between children of graduate and non-graduate parents, and between the rich and poor; home owners and non-owners. This report recommended that education work much more with home and employers to break such intergenerational cycles of poverty and privilege with targeted support for the most disadvantaged pupils and an extended school day. So how now might England move forward? What might England learn from the international debate on the future of education, and from Scotland and Wales about the strategy needed to transition towards the more "Personalised, Smarter, Lifelong Learning" advocated for the 21st century?

Educational Manifestos

Firstly, England clearly needs a new Educational Manifesto and masterplan to set out the Vision, Mission and Sense of Direction that the country needs to pursue to raise the performance of all learners and to "level-up" educational opportunity. With the 2024 British General Election on the horizon and after the PM's pronouncement that education is the "silver bullet" to England's future, there is likely to be a blizzard of educational manifestos promising transformation of the English education system—or its perpetuation. As before, many of them are likely to be drawn up by politicians and their advisors and officials rather than by educationalists themselves. And while such manifestos may well reflect deep-felt principles about education and learning, inevitably they are likely to be framed with a keen eye on electoral presentation by a Westminster elite drawn heavily still from the private education sector. In contrast, as illustrated in Chapter 3, many of the leading educational nations have sought to insulate national educational policy from the political arena and its short-term electoral and media pressures and so provide the stability and continuity needed for a long-term strategy monitored and managed by an independent body. As Richard Gerver (2019) has argued"When you look at the world's most dynamic education systems, they all have something in common: their hunger to learn." The aim is excellence not cynicism; collaboration not competition. They work within a common consensus; a national mission and set of agreed goals whereas in UK, the goals of education are confused and unclear and schools tend to react to top-down policies and decisions divorced from reality. Teachers need to be more self-confident and self-assertive. education needs to put innovation above replication, personal development above drives on performance and efficiency. Schools need to focus on the transition into work and HE where independent learning and adaptation are far more crucial than coaching and grades. While results drives the education machine, retention within and between sectors and in later life, is in fact the key to greater productivity. After all, it is young people today who will change the world tomorrow, not the older generations or the policy-makers of today and yesterday. As China's Ten Regulations for primary pupils pro-claimed in 2013 (Strauss 2013), as educators "we may only touch a young person's life for a brief moment in time, but we must ensure that we contribute to a far longer journey … . Tomorrow is yet to be written and, in the most traditional sense, we need to provide the pen and ink but not the story". So, below are two sample manifestos drawn up by educationalists rather than by political campaigners, manifestos for the long-term, not for the next election, manifestos for the Smart New Age and for All Children and Learners.

The Times Education Commission (TEC)

June 2022 was an Educational Commission called together by the *Times* newspaper to independently examine the state of English education today and look for ways for "Bringing out the Best" and "unleash the potential of every child". Its criticisms of the English education system were sweeping and scathing. A "sausage-machine" and a "bloated and outdated national curriculum"; "a system of education geared to the system, not to the child ... a system (that) is failing on every measure" with the English GCSE examination system the villain of the piece. "The present assessment system has become a dead hand on education that is sucking the energy out of schools, stifling teachers and condemning too many young people to the scrap heap". Success in education is still measured almost entirely "in academic terms" and by an examination system that pervades the whole purpose and performance of schools and colleges creating failure for many as well as success for the academically abler. "The worship of exams is almost sinister"; and "Ofsted, which is supposed to support schools and teachers, has become a toxic brand"; a reign of terror. Teaching is being driven by compliance not creativity, fear not inspiration. It needs a fundamental shift in trust and power towards greater professional autonomy and far less government intervention. "Inequalities are ingrained from an early age"; "provision is patchy, with the most deprived areas often the least well served by the school system". And instead of levelling the playing field, "the education system is too often entrenching divides".

The Commission called instead for a *leap of imagination,* a leap forward into the future not backwards into the past. "Young people today live, laugh and love in the active and engaging environment of the internet and social media yet they are still taught to be robotic learners-passive recipients of knowledge that is no longer relevant nor received rather than creators of the new ideas and ways of working and living that employers desperately seek and society desperately needs". The best education systems are not looking backwards to the selection and rote-learning of the 1950s but looking forward to the competencies needed for the 21st century and for what the WEF calls the Fourth Industrial Revolution; a revolution of automation, AI, robotics and incessant innovation and disruption alongside the Age of Longevity and need for lifelong learning. In particular, argued the Commission, it is a time to take party politics out of education and move beyond the tired ideological divisions that have for too long driven what and how children learn and devise a system based on the "national interest not ministerial whim". As Rachel Sylvester, Chair of the TEC explained in the *Times* in May 2022 "Britain still has a recognisably 19th century school and university education system, facilitated by 20th century technology, which for all its achievements, is now embarrassingly unfit for purpose in the 21st century ... Social mobility has largely stalled, and the school system tells a third of students that they have failed" while "our students leave school and university lacking the skills that employers have been telling us for years that they need". Students' wider talents and aptitudes—social, artistic, sporting and personal—are often underdeveloped, especially among the less well-off and "many leave the education system incapable of living gainfully and happily in society, as seen by the rise in mental problems among the young". England needs a 15 year strategy drawn up in consultation with business, scientists, cultural figures, local politicians, civic leaders as to what the nation needs "rather than what is in one party's short-term political interest", monitored by a small independent body similar to the OBR.

The Times Education Commission set out a 12-point Plan for Education that included:

- a British Baccalaureate as a much broader and fairer mode of assessment at 18 with a slimmed down mid-stage GCSE assessment based on online tests and continuous assessment as well as formal exams similar to the IB Middle School Certificate offered across the rest of Europe;
- a Smart Learning Strategy based on personalised ipads operated by AI with a dashboard outlining their personal programme of study and monitoring their progress, identifying strengths and weaknesses and reporting to teachers (and parents) as developed by Century Tech; software that can monitor and motivate pupils allowing them to advance at their own pace irrespective of their age and relieving teachers of such traditional administration so supporting the pedagogic shift from the Age of the "Sage on the Stage" to the Age of the "Coach on the Side-line" as students increasingly learn to teach themselves and teach each other;
- a universal National Citizen Service for all pupils at 14, entrepreneurial courses run by local businesses such as "Apprentice for a Day" and partnerships with local public schools to share facilities and extend student tutoring all suggested as means to broaden and engage all pupils irrespective of academic ability;
- a Digital Learner Profile that included a student's outside interests and achievements as well their academic qualifications as a means for schools to develop and publish a far more personalised, holistic and educationally inclusive profile of each pupil/student's character, skills and interests than the paltry list of GCSE grades achieved, or not, achieved at age 16;
- a UPN to identify and track all school pupils so that the existing *Generation of Ghost* pupils, who seem to have disappeared off school-rolls, potentially some £1.8 million at present, might possibly re-appear;
- mapping software such as that by Century Tech by which the performance of all schools in literacy, numeracy and science might be mapped and assessed possibly by a RAG-rating system as part of an

alternative strategy for monitoring school performance to the current system of school league tables and Ofsted inspections;

- a Technology Academy to test EdTech innovations and with upgraded teacher training. In Estonia, China and the USA, for example, 95% of teachers and pupils have laptops compared to 35% in UK;
- Schools as Community Hubs not isolated islands with, as many schools already do, breakfast and after school clubs, on-site social workers and in schools putting themselves and associated social and policing services at the centre of the local community;
- a spotlight on pupils "Out of the Mainstream"; in Special Needs and Disabilities and Alternative Provision; an area providing for some 1.4 million state pupils in England (16% of total) across a huge and very diverse range of needs, many of which were intensified by the pandemic. In particular, the Commission argued for a fundamental shift from viewing children with SEN as abnormal or defective requiring separate or segregated treatment but rather that education embrace the notion that there is no "normal" but rather a rainbow of educational needs and unique talents covering all children of which SEN is simply one element. Autism is now recognised as a talent by organisations as diverse as GCHQ and the gaming industry but one that remains unrecognised in today's education system and disproportionately represented amongst the 30% or so who annually fail the English GCSE. The Commission also highlighted the escalating number of permanent exclusions pre- and post-Covid, the waste of talent involved and the heightened risk of recruitment into crime, poverty and early death at great lifelong cost to society financially and socially. Hence the Commission's call for much higher quality alternative provision (AP) units possibly set up by MATs themselves alongside better quality education in adult prisons as part of an urgent rehabilitation strategy given the levels of illiteracy and innumeracy within a British prison population, one of the largest in Europe;
- a Lifetime Learning Strategy that includes a programme of university building in "cold spot" towns of over 80,000 population as part of its "levelling up" agenda alongside a levelling up of post-16 student funding to support FE in its mission to pick up the "forgotten third" who fall through the school net, an increase in apprenticeships, an inter-sector credit scheme to sit alongside the Government's Lifelong Loan Entitlement to support job transfer and a Lifelong Learning programme as part of a *cradle to grave strategy* for economic prosperity.

This was a massive and all-inclusive summary of the State of the Nation's Education that has rightly attracted considerable attention ever since including PM Sunak's supportive comments in October 2023. In tone and policy thrust, the TEC report looked and felt like "*Education,*

Education, Education" Part 2 and certainly Tony Blair and Andrew Adonis saw it in that light in their submission to the Commission; as part of the permanent revolution in education that New Labour initiated back in 1997–2010. In a follow-up report for the Tony Blair Institute for Global Change (IGC), Steve Coulter and colleagues (2022) focused on three specific areas of reform in implementing the TEC recommendations, namely:

1 Pupil Assessment and School Performance reform by scrapping the Ebacc, introducing elements of the four 21CS using the emerging OECD measures and replacing the current GCSE/A-level qualification system with a new baccalaureate-style qualification at age 18 and a series of low-stake tests at 16 to inform pupil choice and hold schools to account.
2 School Inspection reform by shifting the nature and tone of Ofsted inspections from threats to visits by a "critical friend" using a one-page summary of strengths and weaknesses instead of the current grading system but retaining a pass/fail assessment for failing schools; by establishing a national digital infrastructure for education including a "student-owned learner" ID and digital profile, a designated data body for the schools sector and a peer benchmarking data tool for schools to contextualise performance with Ofsted charged with contextualising and targeting proposed interventions with peer-to-peer expert groups to help resolve intractable problems.
3 Curriculum reform of the national curriculum through an expert commission with a focus on literacy, numeracy, science and eventually digital competency, under the auspices of a non-political independent body to support long-term planning and encourage innovation and best professional practice rather than party-political or ideological intervention.

As the IGC authors concluded "At the core of a reformed system should be a revised curriculum, more sophisticated modes of assessment and a new, rigorous accountability framework that is better attuned to the things that matter most. By pairing this with a comprehensive EdTech strategy, we can personalise learning so that pupils grasp the basics much more quickly ... free up time and introduce the right incentives for a focus on developing more complex skills. That would be a system fit for purpose in an age of profound transformation".

The Fourth Education Revolution

Is Sir Anthony Seldon's personal contribution to the emerging education debate but with a specific focus on the emergence of AI and the 4th Education Revolution, that he believes, is "hurtling towards" all of us. In his view the 4th Educational Revolution is based on six future innovations- transhumanism; robotics; voice and face recognition; quantum computing; cloud computing and collaborative working; internet of things and Big Data. These are emerging innovations that Seldon & Abidoye believe will help to sweep away the "inherent problems of the (educational) factory system" notably its gross social unfairness, its administrative burden on teachers, the narrow range of intelligences and abilities being developed, and students being homogenised not individualised. Instead, these authors believe AI will provide personalised tuition; greater social mobility as type of school and home background becomes less of a determinant; *stage not age* so pupils learn at their pace not the system's; teachers' freedom from admin to teach better and more individually; a greater breadth of intelligences, skills and aptitudes that can be nurtured alongside pupils learning more at their pace and through such techniques as gaming; preparing them for future world of work via VR and AR, and encouraging lifelong learning as a pleasure in itself not just a chore for a qualification or training. They believe that the impact of AI on education will be immense too in driving fundamental change for universities, underpinning the rise of MOOCs and online learning; revolutionising our understanding of learning and the human brain and accelerating the arrival of jobs of the future. They foresee a new six-stage university structure as likely to emerge involving global, national, regional and local universities, professional and digital ones and a radically restructured system of physical and virtual degree accreditation and delivery through smart universities. Schools and teachers, they believe, will still be essential to the future of education but organised more smartly and more personally. If we use AI well, argue Seldon and Abidoye, we will also retain the best of the "third education revolution", notably the social experience, the positive interactions with staff, the stimulating careers for teachers, and the academic ambition and seriousness but equally make education and learning better, much better.

While *The Fourth Educational Revolution* is a powerful manifesto for Smart Learning and an AI revolution within schools and colleges as well as underpinning lifelong learning, Anthony Seldon is certainly not unaware of the dangers of AI. "AI is infinitely seductive. It will know us better than our best friends, our parents, our partners. It probably already does". Currently "we are educating our young to become more like machines, like robots but digital technology and AI machines will always outperform us. Instead we need to be educating our young to become more fully human". If not, we will be "sleep-walking into a world in which AI will impoverish rather than enrich all our lives". Academics such as Professor Neil Selwyn (2016) have been warning about the risks of EdTech/AI infiltration into state education for many years. In Selwyn's view far from new technology "liberalising and democratising" education, it is just as likely to as formal education to reproduce and legitimise inequality as well as create the new inequality of the "digital divide"; or worse lead to educational privatisation by Big Tech as huge corporations from Apple to Pearson's, MS and Google move insidiously into what is fast becoming a multi-million, even multi-billion industry. Selwyn therefore proposes putting it clearly under state regulation, governance and investment; controlling the profit motivation of private enterprise whilst incentivising its engagement and investment through taxes or benefits and ethical and transparency requirements as part of corporate social responsibility and a public–private partnership. "Most of the ways forward do not relate to how digital technology might make public education better, but how public education might make digital technology better" by harnessing it in the pursuit of the values of social justice, equity and democracy so that all benefit not just the wealthier few. Selwyn (2019) is just as cautious about the Robot Revolution looming over the educational horizon. As charming and innocent as classroom robots and chatbots currently are; as super-efficient as modern data management and student support systems may seem to be, they are neither designed by teachers or controlled by them so leaving the potential for them in the future to control teachers and their students rather than the other way round. This would be professionally disempowering, relegating teachers into becoming merely the agents and operatives of learning systems that they never designed nor have ultimate control over; or undergo the sort of radical workforce restructuring that has happened in other industries. While AI may herald a new era of educational efficiency, the price over time of losing the very independence and objectivity that is the existential core of western democratic culture; its capacity to critique and challenge ethical and ideological assumptions as part of free speech is under potential threat. It fears like this that led the House of Lords Liaison Committee Report AI in the UK (2020) to recommend that the government urgently create an AI Council, a Code of AI Ethics, a national retraining scheme for AI retraining and transition and appoint a Chief Data Officer at Cabinet level to champion AI use in public services in a safe and principled way; a recommendation that may see the full light of the techno-day in the current government's proposal for an AI Institute to predict and oversee AI development and security.

Certainly, AI in the UK is moving forward at pace. HM Government has a National AI Strategy (2021) and an ambition to make the UK a "global superpower in AI" through a 10-year investment plan. The Department for Education has plans for driving "improvements in educational outcomes" (2019) and for supporting the development of a "vibrant EdTech business sector" (2022) producing high-quality products that meet the needs of educators and foster a pipeline of fresh ideas with a series of innovation competitions, a testbed of schools and colleges piloting and trialling new developments. Demonstrator schools and colleges will set out best practice, a National Retraining Scheme is planned to help adults at risk from automation needing retraining and an EdTech Leadership Group representing both industry and education is proposed to drive this agenda forward under a new EdTech Agreement scheduled for the end of the year. This report cites such pockets of good practice as Bolton Colleges' virtual assistant AIDA, Ark MAT's use of the Cloud, Wolverhampton University's virtual dissection technology and Highfurlong Special School's assistive technology. The JISC report on AI in tertiary education (April 2021) illustrates similar examples of innovation and best practice in Further Education.

Such grand plans, however, contrast starkly with the realities of everyday school life. As the Department's survey by Cooper Gibson Research (2021) illustrated while COVID-19 dramatically brought forward the supply and use of EdTech in schools with remote learning and the Oak National Academy curriculum, most schools still do not have an EdTech investment strategy in place for teaching and learning and the obstacles to Edtech adoption continue to centre around the cost of and funding for EdTech especially in state schools, alongside staff knowledge of and trust in EdTech products and their lack of confidence in using EdTech, notably amongst older staff. Simply recruiting technical staff or specialist expertise into education for such fast-moving EdTech applications is a major challenge in itself while the "digital poverty" amongst disadvantaged households is accelerating educational and economic inequality. Data privacy and system security are major concerns and the complexity of many systems has put a lot of staff off; although the Tribal platform was cited as simplicity itself with "absolutely everything literally on one page". While exams remain primarily pen and paper, some exam boards are now exploring online testing. So, EdTech research and experimentation in schools in England are still advancing at "walking pace" although reliable comparison sites like EdTech and EdSurge are starting to emerge as the EdTech market surges towards the $404 billion predicted for 2025. Here, two main markets appear to be opening up: B2B (business to business) direct with education sector; and B2C indirectly with consumers such as learners and parents. VR and AR were the largest areas of EdTech spend in 2018 but by 2025 AI is expected to be dominant as it deepens and advances especially in testing and assessment. Meanwhile, blockchain has the potential to transform educational certification, security, finance and data management while VR is already allowing greater immersive learning and the environment for students to practice and display their skills safely with "serious gaming" already becoming an arena for students to perform 21CS in "real-life-type scenarios" using for example,

the World Bank's EVOKE game or Foldlt games as "citizen scientists".
Social Robots are emerging too as potential and personalised learning
aids, as teaching assistants, peer learners and digital avatars not only
helping pupils who have fallen behind but giving lectures to the whole
class and assisting with daily administration such as student registration.
AI may be seen as the great gamechanger in education, but, as outlined
in Chapter 2, the escalating fear is that it is potentially outstripping
human control as so many countries still lack a clear AI strategy or the
underpinning infrastructure to make its adoption consistent across
platforms. Hence the international AI Summit was held at Bletchley
Park in the UK in November 2023.

Towards an Educational Framework for the Future

"An education system is not successful because of tests and output-driven
hurdles; it is successful when individuals are recognized and the diversity
of their talent is celebrated. It is successful when students are (happy)
and fulfilled and (go onto) to live fulfilling lives". (Robinson 2016)

So, what might an English Educational Framework fit for the
21st century actually look like and how might it be delivered effectively
and sustainably; what might an education system that is not only
Personalised, Smarter and Life-Long but one that is also All-Inclusive
supporting All children, the whole child and nothing but the child (or
adult) in their lifelong educational journey in the 21st century. This would
involve a philosophical and strategic shift from selecting the ablest and
moulding the rest towards ensuring that *every child matters* and none must
be left behind; one where schools and colleges are not educational factories
but as Ken Robinson (2016/2022) has consistently argued, nurseries
nurturing the learning, personal skills, talents and motivation of each
and every student and where the whole structure of education in England
is turned on its head so that the system is designed, measured and funded
to ensure that no child falls through, fails or is cast aside. A paradigm shift
exemplified by countries such as Japan and especially Singapore, a country
that has transformed its education system from one of the toughest exam
regimes in the world into one of the tenderest. Such a paradigm shift would
require what the Learning Policy Institute (2020) has described as a *Re-
Imagination*: a reimagination of the whole of the English education system,
its purpose and its architecture:

• Re-imagining the Learner of the Future and his/her individual and
  collective needs, talents and ambitions, personalising learning and
  nurturing the potential and personal development of **all** students
  irrespective of background not just the privileged few or even the
  advantaged many; and nurturing within all learners a *Growth Mindset*;

an ambition, motivation and resilience to grow and progress as an individual and as a member of the community while profiling the educational and personal progression of each and every student through a Life Long Learning portfolio.

- Re-imagining the Teacher of the Future, his/her role within a redesigned teaching workforce in promoting and supporting learning alongside new pedagogy, new technology and possibly a new school–home environment.
- Re-Imagining and redesigning the curriculum of the future and incorporating *into* it—not just alongside it— such life-long 21CS skills as creativity, critical thinking, communication and collaboration alongside decision making, digital literacy, entrepreneurship and emotional intelligence.
- Re-Imagining Innovation and the integration of AI and new technology in supporting learning, learning support and digital profiling.
- Re-Imagining and elevating the Voice and Engagement of students—and parents—in a partnership of learning and learning support.
- Re-Imagining Educational Partnerships with parents, employers and the local community as underpinning clear and integrated Progression Pathways across the educational sectors and into the world of work and 21st-century life.

The changes above reflect both the education manifestos above and put together they represent a fundamental shift for English education; a paradigm shift in focus and inclusion; a shift:

- From mass education (age 5–24) monopolised by educational institutions to personalised learning for life (age 3–100); from centralised national systems of education to more devolved educational and learning partnerships; from learning limited to place and time to learning anywhere, anytime and across the world via the Internet.
- From the narrow, academic based curriculum of today to broader skills-based curriculum of tomorrow; one where personal qualities and capabilities are acknowledged and accredited as highly as academic knowledge and skills; one where knowledge and understanding of the outside world is as important as the academic learning nurtured within the educational world.
- From terminal examinations at ages such as 16 and 18 with on-time, online tests not just of academic knowledge but ongoing skill mastery and application in real-life projects or scenarios involving such issues as health and well-being, climate change and social media.
- From age-related testing to life-long personalised profiling and skill development; a Baccalaureate of progressive learning rather than a series of age-related terminal grades.

- From teacher-led learning to a learning partnership, with students acting as mentors, innovators and trainers while teachers operate more as coaches and learning managers.
- From learning at a desk in a classroom to learning at a laptop across the internet. From learning alone to learning as part of a team; a team that might include avatars, AI and robotic tutors particularly for students with special needs, disabilities or from disadvantaged backgrounds.
- From managing education and learning through the competitive chaos and fragmentation of a market-based school system to new models of public organisation, funding and partnership that enhance the status and power of teachers as professionals, reward teamwork, innovation and enterprise.
- From schools as inward and isolated institutions to schools as learning and community hubs for all ages 24/7 responding to broader local communities needs for learning, child-care, eldercare in an ageing and technology-based society.
- From managing education directly through a political authority and centralised bureaucracy to creating a new independent National Education Authority or Steering Group similar say to the Bank of England (BoE) and Office for Budget Responsibility (OBR) not to manage English Education but to monitor and steer it on the basis of an agreed 10 year National Education Plan and so liberate English education from party political, electoral and ministerial "swings and roundabouts".

Achieving this shift, articulating a new Educational Vision and redesigning the strategic aims, ambitions and architecture of an education system as entrenched in inequality as in England will be an educational and political challenge of immense proportions that will test the political skill of even the most seasoned of politicians and the political commitment and endurance of more than one governing administration. However, the forthcoming British General Election offers an ideal platform for debating the need for fundamental change and the potential pathways to it. It equally throws-up the question about the political mechanism best needed to undertake it once a new administration is in power. The usual strategy is to appoint a Chair and an Educational Commission similar to the TEC but with representation not only from the great and the good, educationalists and employers but possibly teachers, parents and students speaking from the "shop floor". The selection of a Chair would be crucial to its credibility and its task in drafting a New Educational Vision and Implementation Plan (2025–2035) as well as the management structure needed to lead, monitor and oversee it over a protracted period of 10 years or more, reviewed and overseen like the rest of the UK by an international observer such as the OECD. This would be a massive exercise and as Scotland and Wales have learnt, not an easy one. So is there a **"Third Way"**, an alternative possibly more evolutionary than revolutionary strategy; one that incorporates all the proposals above but instead of dismantling and replacing the whole English educational edifice, simply redirects the existing one from its current focus on selection to one embracing inclusion; a *stealth strategy* that gives the existing structure new life and a new mission with school and classroom leaders given the trust and responsibility of transforming future English education on the basis of a new philosophy and educational master-plan. This would initiate a new relationship between government and education, a new partnership between politicians and schools; a shift from control and compliance from above to mutual trust and working together as apparently works so well in the leading nations internationally and as the next step recommended for Scotland and Wales; a strategy empowering the education sector with incentives and trust rather than direction and disruption and one with changes in stages rather than attempting to redesign it all in one go. Below are six possible stages by which such a stealth strategy might be undertaken.

Stage One: *Redesigning and Broadening the English National Curriculum & Assessment system to make it more personalised and all-inclusive.*

Step 1 would involve discarding the E'bacc and its academic stranglehold on the 14–16 curriculum and so release the potential for learning of the creative, technical and social subjects previously excluded from the Progress 8 measure. Secondly, broaden the purely academic nature of the English national curriculum by re-opening the 14–19 curriculum in partnership with FE to vocational and occupational courses and qualifications as operated with the day-release programmes between schools and colleges in the 1980s. Thirdly, incorporate some or all of the 21CS into schools' Extra-Curricular Programmes so enabling all pupils of all talents and interests to enjoy and gain accreditation for activities that interest them and help them develop personally whether it be sports leadership or DoE. Expanding and redesigning the school curriculum in this way, would, in many ways, take it back to the much broader 14–19 curriculum offered before the e'bacc and incentivise schools in developing and strengthening working partnerships with local colleges, employers and community groups. While such a step is likely to require additional funding as well as "encouragement" from Ofsted, it is equally likely to be supported by schools and staff seeking to offer a much broader, more inclusive and more motivating offer than the restricted one of today.

Step 2 designing and trialling a British Baccalaureate (BB); a daunting task on first sight but made much easier by the fact that the International Baccalaureate (IB) is not a new and untested qualification but an established and highly respected curriculum model used across most of Europe and in over 200 schools and colleges in the UK today. The IB framework is seen by many educationalists as a proven example of the sort of Curriculum Framework needed for 21st-century learning given its breadth and depth, philosophy of independent learning, its progressive learning structure for all ages, its international reputation for quality and rigour and its widespread acceptance by universities and employers. Most critically, the IB has its own in-built assessment and qualification framework so negating the need for replacing GCE and A-level systems and trialling a new alternative; a mammoth task in itself and one that is likely to spark strong opposition from a "standards lobby" that has dominated, if not dictated, education in England since the 1970s. Finally, research such as that by Katie Wright and her colleagues (2015) seems to indicate that not only is the IB potentially a life-changing learning experience but that it seems to have a profound and life-lasting effect on student's career and personal development thereafter. It encourages international-mindedness, critical thinking, positive dispositions to lifelong learning and self-confidence as well as enhancing university and job applications. It also offers an IB alumni network that students might turn to throughout life. Most especially, according to TN Hopenbeck and her colleagues (2021), the IB Career-related Programme (CP) "provides the prospect of better life opportunities for a generation of students from less privileged backgrounds".

Helpfully the National Baccalaureate Trust (NBT: 2022) has recently proposed a phased model by which existing qualifications such as GCSEs and A-levels can be incorporated into (or be offered alongside) the Baccalaureate framework as a first step towards a full-scale British Baccalaureate with the opportunity at a later date to extend the IB framework down into middle and primary education. The NBT believes that the baccalaureate framework would offer all pupils and all students full accreditation of their level of achievement and a record of their personal development rather than just those who pass at a certain grade. The NBT's UNiVERSAL leaver's award, in turn, is designed to acknowledge ALL young peoples' achievements, broaden the 14–19 curriculum and overcome the traditional academic-technical divide. Under the NBT framework a British Baccalaureate could be delivered in two parts: Part One 14–16 and Part Two 16–18, comprising core learning including English and Maths and Personal Development and an Independent Extended Project (IEP), with a tiered accreditation system of 200 credits in Part One and 400 credits in Part Two. The Core Learning sections in Parts One and Two could, respectively, incorporate GCSEs, A-levels, T-Levels, BTecs as required as well as accrediting the IEP and such community activities as the DOE Award, work experience, creative arts and community service at Level 1, 2 and 3 or Foundation, Intermediate and Advanced. Integrating assessment within the curriculum rather than outside it, as at present, would at last fulfil Sir Kenneth Baker's directive when designing the English National Curriculum that the assessment process "should be an integral part of the educational process" not a bolt-on addition at the end as with today's GCSEs and SATs.

So the notion of a British Baccalaureate offers huge advantages in terms of its breadth, inclusivity, and integrated assessment system. It does not require the creation of a completely new curriculum and assessment structure and it is already in practice very successfully in schools and colleges across the UK. As Tom Bewick, CEO of the Federation of Awarding Bodies, has commented while the education sector is still suffering from "reform fatigue", "we do not have to completely reinvent the wheel" if it is possible to simply "flex up the existing system to potentially achieve the same aims as a baccalaureate". In fact, schools and colleges could simply adopt the IB themselves, possibly alongside GCSEs and A-levels. It doesn't need a Departmental directive or new legislation. Such a staged change would equally meet the concerns raised by commentators such as Sam Freedman, an ex-No 10 advisor, about the potential impact of the often unintended consequences of educational change As he has pointed out (Aug. 2022) "secondary assessment in the highly centralised English system is particularly high stakes and multi-purposed" simultaneously testing young people, assessing their suitability for FE and HE and holding schools to account for performance. Freedman, therefore, counsels strongly against radical or sudden wholesale change.

Step 3   Introducing—or   reintroducing—a   National   Record   of Attainment & Development (NRAD); an electronic successor to the NRA or National Record of Achievement of the 1980s that would allow students themselves to regularly update, reflect on and so take greater ownership of their learning. Many universities already have such electronic profiles to help students develop their CVs for future applications while a national NRA would ensure that all learning from age 5 to 25 could be profiled and extended into a lifelong record of qualifications and skills for future employment and personal development. Such a personalised record would equally encourage as well as record and accredit, schools Extra-Curricular Activities (ECA) programmes, 21CS and students' personal development as well as provide an educational passport for future progression and applications. It may equally encourage and underpin the sort of staff remodelling that many sixth-form colleges use with their senior tutor system to provide personalised tutoring alongside personalised learning with a team of specialist tutors able to deliver and assess specialist ECA or PHSE short-skill programmes within and between schools and in conjunction with employers and community groups. Most important, such a document might enable schools and colleges to celebrate their graduates not just on leaving but on progressing; not just when they graduate from school and college but how and where they progress to thereafter. Progression is, after all, the ultimate purpose of education and training not just in terms of career or jobs but in terms too of personal development. It is arguably an even more important indicator of educational success than exam performance and should therefore possibly be adopted as a key performance measure. The publication of a national survey of pupil and student destinations post-16/18/25— with individual reports for each school and college—would undoubtedly elevate Progression within the Education Debate and encourage school-employer and HE progression partnerships where few currently exist. The absence of any form of progression tracking within the English state school system sits in stark contrast to the progression pathways developed by England's public schools for propelling their pupils into top universities and top occupations. That after all is their USP and market appeal. A National Record of Attainment and Development (NRAD) would offer English state schools a similar opportunity not only to record the progression of their pupils, past and present, but to celebrate their achievements when they graduate and so publicise more widely the value they have added to each and every child's learning and development. Such a system of student self-reflection might equally provide the vehicle for developing and accrediting the *Growth Mindset* so strongly advocated by the OECD and practiced by nations such as Estonia and Singapore and so be of particular benefit to less advantaged pupils and students in highlighting and profiling their particular talents; actual or latent.

Stage Two: *Developing a new Educational Workforce Plan, Recruitment & Training strategy*, one that reflects the high status of teachers in such leading lights as Singapore and Estonia; one that reflects the pedagogic shift in teaching and learning roles and the new skill sets required in future education; one that reflects the technical and training needed to accommodating new technology, AI and even classroom robots in the teaching and learning process ahead. One, in particular, that reflects the challenges in rewarding, retaining and empowering teachers as well as the need to recruit more widely and in later life in an era of educational change and restricted public service budgets. A new educational workforce plan would equally provide an opportunity to reconsider and reframe the traditional teacher-centric one not only in light of the entry of AI and classroom robots but in terms too of the balance between teaching and tutoring, learning and support. As the 2023 Tutoring Trust Report highlighted the impact of CV-19 has been traumatic as well as dramatic and it still lingers long after the trauma of lockdown. Hence the Trust's call a "Tutoring Guarantee" for every disadvantaged and SEN pupil aged 5–19 who needs additional support for continued academic catch-up; at a cost the Trust estimates of around £290 million per year for NTP, as well as a continuation of around £95 m for 16–19 tuition funding.

Stage Three: *Reorientating the School Accountability system* from compliance and conformity to improvement and innovation. Like the TEC report, the EDSK report on Ofsted in 2019 recommended that Ofsted shift from its current report template to a 12-point School Information Card (SIC) the sort of one-page summary of key findings and traffic lights used in the USA in districts such as North Carolina and Washington; one in which there is no overall grade, but like Scotland and Wales, an assessment of the validity and reliability of individual schools self-evaluation strategies; strategies ideally measured against external benchmarks and undertaken by independent evaluators if substantive and sustained self-improvement is likely to be achieved. The OECD's PISA-schools model offers schools and colleges a framework for self-evaluation and benchmarking internationally. Alternatively or additionally, national monitoring as elsewhere in Europe, could be undertaken by national sampling of pupil performance.

Stage Four: *The adoption, adaption and integration of new Smart Teaching, Learning and Administrative technology into schools and colleges* that advocates believe will both liberate teachers from unnecessary administrative burdens and incite learning innovation across the curriculum. This would need to include updating and upskilling staff on AI developments and introducing innovations such as classroom robots on the basis of national guidance and secure codes of practice from approved EdTech providers through regional technology test centres and training schools, seed-funded and incentivized by new government money and national development deadlines. Sponsorship by and collaboration between business and education would need to be encouraged but under strict and transparent guidelines to ensure that such partnerships prioritise the public good and staff and student safety not corporate profit.

Stage Five: *Redesigning and Restructuring the English State School System 5-16/18 and its post-16 sector.* This clearly a much longer-term and political project with intense debates likely to arise about the future architecture of English education and whether it returns to a revitalised local government control or remains under the existing MAT system with the shift towards larger regional MATs and greater accountability suggested in recent legislation. In the immediate and short-term, however, most of the changes listed above can be accommodated within the existing structure. In fact, Multi-Academy Trusts were originally charged with being engines of innovation and freed from external control to do so. Few have taken this opportunity but in theory, they already have all the powers that they need to lead and drive such innovations given the suitable encouragement, funding and incentives. In this way, and against national deadlines, MATS could be required to become:

- more inclusive and, by incorporation or partnership, offer the full range of provision 5–19 with appropriate courses and support for all abilities from the academically able through to those with SEN, ADHD or special talents or personality types that require specialist support or external provision;
- deliver the Baccalaureate Curriculum and NRAD proposed above;
- take responsibility for the introduction, implementation and development of Smart Learning and Administration through their own in-house innovation unit or through external support from a national or regional Education and Innovation Unit;
- design an appropriate and cost-effective Workforce Model for recruiting, retaining and rewarding high-quality teaching and technical staff;
- install and implement a Quality Assurance system based on the mantra of *"every child matters"* and capable of personalising pupil progress not only academically but across the 21CS.
- create working partnerships with colleges, employers and public schools to support curriculum delivery and student progression and employability;
- create and engage with educational partnerships in the UK and Europe to support baccalaureate delivery as well as offer pupils/ students experience and staff placements abroad.

In the longer term, however, the MAT model of school management is open to debate. As the EDSK Report Trust Issues (2019) argued the DfE Trust programme has created a parallel state school system with unaccountable Trusts running alongside accountable local authority schools creating "a fragmented educational system with little sign of improvement" or benefit to pupils despite "the considerable energy" expended by politicians and civil servants in maintaining this system instead of focusing on whether the Trust system actually improves outcomes. Numerous concerns have been raised about the governance and financial accountability of Trusts including CEO pay, conflicts of interest and selective admissions policies. The current patchwork of school systems is indefensible in the long run but it may, as suggested above, be amenable to modification and proper oversight rather than undergo yet another national restructuring if, but only if, it can prove itself to be the "engine of change" needed in delivering the above agenda for all pupils not just the select few.

Similarly, any wholesale educational restructuring debate must not just be about schools but about the whole of post-16/18 education and lifelong learning thereafter. This would be the opportunity to bring the educational "Cinderella" of English education, FE out of the shadows and into the light as an equal partner alongside its "ugly sisters", the school and university sectors, providing and promoting lifelong learning and Progression Pathways 16–60. However, at present FE in England lacks the identity and clarity of focus of schools and universities. It still tends to be seen as all things to all students. Hence the ESK Report's proposal (2020) that FE be restructured and rebadged as three separate and distinct post-16 sections; namely, Community Colleges, Sixth-Form Colleges and Technology Colleges, each with a clear and distinct offer and progression pathway supported by investment in new buildings and infrastructure and funded by the Individual Education Budgets (IEB) proposed by EDSK in 2019. The FEA: Opportunity England Report (2023) strongly endorses the idea of FE as the flagship for Lifelong Learning post-16 with a curriculum for all, a statutory right to Lifelong Learning, and a national post-16 education and skills strategy to support local communities and their economies. Finally, as outlined in Chapter 3, British universities across the UK are having to reconsider their future role, structure and market strategy, and if necessary reposition themselves in the fast-moving arena of post-18 and lifetime learning.

Certainly, creating a Progression Map from cradle to grave for pupils and students today in the UK would be an "eye-opening" exercise likely to bring out into the light the disarray described by Professor Ball in his 2018 lecture. Certainly, there is a real need for a simple diagram to help learners progress from A to B in the "alphabet soup" that is the English education. Individual institutions, like schools and colleges, tend to focus almost exclusively on their own institutional or sector performance with relatively limited knowledge of how the whole schema fits together or even where their pupils or students go onto next even though preparation for progression is the very heart of learning for the future. Education tomorrow will be a lifelong journey. Your qualifications, as Gillian Keegan, the Education Secretary, might have commented, are simply your ticket to the next station or stage; a journey into the unknown that is now the 21st century; one that will contain multiple twists and turns, blind alleys and even U-turns but one that all students today will need to learn to navigate, will need "to learn, unlearn and re-learn" and possess the resilience and mindset to do so if they are to be successful. A National Survey of Student Progression would undoubtedly illuminate the hazy jungle of the life ahead as well as enlighten older generations with rosy memories of school days long past to recognising the immense and existential challenges facing younger generations today and tomorrow. A new series of *7 Up* might equally help inform and update public opinion about the life chances of those who "fall off the map"; those who "fail" or were excluded from the current education system as to why fundamental reform is so urgently needed; an Educational Journey and Roadmap with a David Attenborough-like figure pointing out the pitfalls as well as the promises of the current system, the opportunities and the challenges ahead and the alternative routeways for learning in the future.

A new 7 Up series of school children past and present would also illuminate the relationship of private and public education; of public school pathways into HE and employment compared to those available to state school and college pupils and students. The independent sector in the English education system is tiny in size, a mere 7% of the school population, yet one of the most powerful and protected given the positions of power held by its graduates past and present. Its elite and privileged status has attracted intense criticism and numerous proposals for reform or abolition; proposals ranging from total abolition and the removal of charity status to the Labour Party's current proposal to add VAT to private school fees. However, as Francis Green and David Kynaston have argued (2019) while public opinion overwhelmingly agrees that private education offers an unfair and lifetime advantage to the wealthiest in society and exceptional access to power and privilege not seen in other major economies, outlawing private education completely would generate a political storm that neither Britain's political parties, nor probably the general public, have much appetite for. Partnership especially in terms of access to facilities and integration of public and state school pupils in ECA programmes in partnership with Employers and HE might be the more beneficial and inclusive way to go.

Stage Six: *Education funding*: a minefield on its own but the fuel that drives the whole education engine, the direction it takes and at what pace. As Paul Johnson (2023) and the IFS have argued, educational funding in the UK needs a fundamental overhaul and remodelling; a long and tortuous task but one that as shown in Further Education in the 1990s when colleges became incorporated, can have profound effects in incentivising growth, and in focusing attention not only on the recruitment of students but on their retention; not only on the attractiveness of the courses on offer but on the size and value of individual students programmes of study *on entry, on course & on exit*. One alternative to completely redesigning the current national funding formula for the post-18 sector, is Tom Richmond's proposal (EDSK: 2019) of a system of Individual Education Budgets or IEBs. In his view "Our post-18 education system is broken" with outstanding student debt already over £100 billion and forecast to reach £450 bn by 2050. Instead, he recommends a shift from student loans to Individual Educational Budgets (IEBs) for young people and adults; a "learning account" of £20,000 to be spent on education and training with the precise sum dependent on such factors as personal background and household income, level of course or training etc. This is a similar system to countries such as Singapore, Sweden, France and the Netherlands and one that might support lifelong learning as well as post-18 education and training right through from level 2 to level 8 (Phd). Each IEB would have a lifetime loan limit of £75,000, once the initial government funds have been depleted. Such as system puts control of learning much more in the hands of learners rather than providers and government, tilts the tertiary system in favour of the more disadvantaged as most courses would not cost more than the £20,000 initially donated by the Government. In Tom Richmond's view, such a radical shift could underpin the whole tertiary education system from universities to colleges and apprenticeships in a far fairer and more cost-effective way, saving potentially some £2.7 billion a year according to EDSK estimates. It would however require a high quality Careers and Course Advisory Service to support student choice and a strict Quality Assurance regime to prevent fraud and maintain its public and political credibility.

Implementation

This six-stage strategy for educational reform has obvious advantages compared to the "root & branch" approach proposed elsewhere.

The "stealth strategy" above does not require the hefty leadership and management apparatus used in other national transformation programmes. It could, if approved, even be executed in the initial stages by schools themselves with MATs made accountable for leading and managing this initiative, operating under a National Masterplan with an agreed timetable and a funding regime that rewarded successful innovation; a national partnership between government and education aimed at enabling schools and colleges to own and drive change rather than have it thrust upon them. The "wheel does not have to reinvented", but it would require the Educational Sector and its member institutions to adopt a fundamentally different educational mission and mode of working to ensure that every learner has a fulfilling educational experience, gets to where they need to go and develops the 21CS and mindset to successfully navigate the future. This would require clear leadership, guidance and strict monitoring from above and a funding regime that incentivised high quality and transferable innovation based on student success and value for public money supported by a new education workforce plan and salary system to attract the best into teaching and trust them to deliver as in best practice elsewhere. Many of the OECD recommendations for Scotland and Wales are represented in this proposal and below is a possible timetable for such a staged change but with the proviso that several of these initiatives could be accelerated or compressed into shorter timeframes with institutions encouraged to take the initiative and lead innovation rather than wait to follow:

Phase One (2024–2026): Design, Debate and Experimentation

The creation of an All-Party Education Commission to draft a 10 Year Educational Vision, Mission and Strategic Plan for English Education long-term; a plan to be put out for public consultation ideally with all-party support and a revised model of educational policy-making and implementation that includes a new educational body similar to the Office for Budget Responsibility (OBR) to advise, guide and rebrief the DfE. This is likely to include a new funding regime designed to drive proven innovation and value for money (VFM); a new or revised accountability regime designed on one hand to support and encourage school-based self-assessment against a published reporting template and external verification and on the other to develop a system of annual performance sampling similar to that used elsewhere and in tune with the OECD PISA model to allow to for direct international comparisons. Judging by the experiences of Scotland and Wales, there is clearly value too in engaging the OECD in a regular system review.

Meanwhile, MATs are well positioned in this first phase, with guidance and funding incentives from the DfE and encouragement from Ofsted, to become engines of school innovation, initiating and experimenting with one or more of the proposals above; be that introducing the IB into one or more of their member schools, adopting or developing an electronic personalised pupil portfolio or NRAD, expanding its curriculum offer to provide vocational courses 14–19 in partnership with local FE colleges and/or expanding the schools ECA offer and incorporating and profiling students 21CS in partnership with local employers, charities and public schools. Enlarged MATs also offer the opportunity for a wider range of internal provision and expertise in SEN and pupil wellbeing needs, possibly through a specialist unit or the "alternative provision" that many local councils currently struggle to provide. MATs, provided that they are of a certain range, size and specialism 11–19 or 5–19, are in a strong position therefore to provide the sort of devolved and local leadership practised in Estonia and Scandinavia, empowering schools and teachers to re-own the curriculum and position themselves as key players in any future educational landscape rather than remain the "foot-soldiers" of a discredited market-based ideology from the early 2000s.

Phase Two (2026–2029): National Implementation

England moves nationally to a new British Baccalaureate and assessment system based say on the stages proposed by the National Baccalaureate Trust along with:

- a new personalised and electronic portfolio of pupil skills, attainment and progression supported by a structured tutoring system;
- the initial stages of a school-based EdTech strategy led by DfE guidance, supported by enterprise funding, protected by codes of best practice and advised by independent "Which-style" advisory bodies and localised EdTech test-beds in schools, colleges or employers such as BT.

Phase Three (2029–2035): Review and Revision

The English educational landscape is remapped based on Lifelong Learning (LLL), the impact of new learning technology and online training and accreditation. These remapped Progression Pathways would integrate early and school education (5–19) with Technical and Higher education and onto Lifelong Learning Skills Centres located throughout each region with both specialist and general options and reskilling based on the local and national economy in partnership with local employers and specialist career advisers. FE colleges, technical universities and community schools could clearly host and deliver such courses and qualifications funded by the Individual Learning Accounts proposed by ESK above and practised in Singapore and elsewhere. While this stage may sound like an educational HS2 project, in many ways it is unravelling the opaque and tangled educational web that currently afflicts English state and further education to make it more transparent, accessible and supportive of the sort of lifelong learning and reskilling the 21st century is already demanding and so bring English education out from the "splendid isolation" of the past into becoming the educational hub serving the whole community not just the academically abler and in moving from a middling position internationally into becoming a world leader.

This is clearly a massive and challenging educational regeneration programme but as the London Challenge showed, where there is the political and national will and consistency of purpose, ambition and leadership, there is a way, provided education feels trusted and has greater ownership of its future, committed to its delivery by professional pride rather than external compliance and inspection. Just as Singapore shifted dramatically in 2006 from being a high-pressure system focused almost exclusively on test scores, so perhaps with educationalists in the driving seat, England too can also *"Teach Less and Learn More"*, can shift from a test and teacher-centric focus onto a student centred one where the curriculum focuses on being able to apply knowledge not just absorb and regurgitate it, where subject choice is broader but content reduced, where progression pathways are clearer and of equal value and where, as in Singapore, there is a chain of "Future Schools & Colleges" to showcase a vision of the future where acquiring 21CS such as teamwork, problem-solving and critical thinking are not only on display supported by integrated digital technology but available for schools and staff to adopt and put into practice.

Finally, any future vision of English education has to be both inspiring and heartfelt throughout and beyond the education sector. It needs to inspire our children and students: all of them not just the academically abler or advantaged. As countries such as Singapore, Japan and Estonia have proudly declared, our children—*all our children*—are our future and we cannot afford economically, socially or morally to lose a single one in early age or later life. While England's present system annually casts aside nearly a third of our children as educational "failures" at the tender age of 16, any future system must include and nurture every last talent not just for the individuals sake but for societies sake or else everyone suffers from the resultant social cost, the loss of economic productivity, the social discontent and political alienation. "Every Child Matters" and none can be lost; every child has talent and creativity and a contribution to make. As the late Ken Robinson (2016/2022) so eloquently put it: *"Children and young people are not impartial by-products of education ... They are the very reason the system exists in the first place". They need nurturing not processing; they need support and direction into a life that far from being smooth and straightforward is likely to be "chaotic, a living game of snakes & ladders, of ups &*

downs, false starts and new directions, of chances taken and opportu-
nities lost". "Life is complex and unpredictable, and because of our
powers of imagination and creativity, we are able to navigate it
(successfully or otherwise)".

Finally, Reflections on a Personal Journey through 40 Years of
Educational Change

This book has been real "blast from the past"; remembering and
reliving a professional and personal journey through the educational
challenges of the past 40 years; a educational rollercoaster across four
counties (Essex, Merseyside, Nottingham and Suffolk) from teaching
in an Educational Priority Area (EPA) on Merseyside, to opening a
new Federated Sixth-Form in the coastal town of Felixstowe,
becoming Vice-Principal of a new post-16 Tertiary College in
Basildon, Essex, on the very same day that the Conservative
Government introduced Direct-Grant Schools so effectively removing
the college's A-level intake and its tertiary status, to becoming
Principal of a Sixth-Form College in Nottingham just as New
Labour came into power. 1997–2010 was an era of significant
educational energy and investment that enabled us to completely
rebuild Bilborough College in Nottingham through the Building
Schools for the Future programme, to drive up results dramatically,
to triple our intake through the new FE funding formula and to
expand the curriculum by introducing the IB alongside an extensive
A-level offer working in partnership with a European Consortium of
Colleges from Sweden, Germany, Poland and France. A truly uplifting
and inspiring experience in educational change and transformation
but one that took ten long years to execute. Leading and managing
the New Labour 14–19 Reform Strategy back in rural Suffolk was
a totally different experience and environment. It involved engaging
and enthusing schools and colleges across the county to form partnerships for delivering the new 14–19 Curriculum and although the
14–19 Diploma programme died with the election of the Coalition
Government and appointment of Michael Gove as Education
Secretary, Suffolk at least inherited nearly £100 million worth of
new post-16 buildings with colleges and skills centres created in some
of its most deprived and rural areas. Suffolk One in Ipswich remains an
outstanding example today of the much broader 16–19 tertiary education
that should be on offer across the country.

So, both my current research and past professional experience have
highlighted the potential for radical educational change but equally,
the immense obstacles in introducing and embedding it into an English

education system that appears to be politically and educationally unstable, elitist and exclusive by design while attempting to "patch-over" the *yawning gap in disadvantage* that remains a hallmark of English society even today. While Educational Manifestos like that by the Times Education Commission and by think-tanks such as Tony Blair's Institute for Global Change offer serious potential blueprints for radical reform 11–16 and beyond, as Scotland and Wales have shown, even with educational visions that the OECD has trumpeted as inspirational, both countries national reform programmes have stuttered, stalled and required major surgery. Hence, the proposal above that England adopt a much more staged and locally managed reform programme; one that engages, incentivises and inspires the education sector and over which they feel both ownership and empowerment in a similar way to the teaching professions in such leading "beacons" of educational light as Finland, Estonia and Singapore-and soon, hopefully Scotland and Wales. Hence too, this book and my undying thanks to a profession and a career that has given me immense satisfaction and professional pride in working with so many great staff and many inspiring pupils and students across the country.

Bibliography

Auditor General for Wales: The New Curriculum for Wales (May 2022)

Auger Philip: *The post-16 Education Review*: House of Commons Library (May 2018)

Biesta Gert: Putting the World in the Centre: A Different Future for Scotland's Education: Scottish Education Review: 1–21 (2023)

Blair A & Hague W: *A New National Purpose: Innovation Can Power the Future of Britain: Jeegar Kakkad et al*: Tony Blair Institute for Global Change (2023)

Blair A & Adonis A: *Education, Education, Education: Submission to TEC*: Tony Blair Institute for Global Change (IGC) (June 2021)

Care Ester et al: *Education System Alignment for 21st Century Skills: Focus on Assessment*: Brookings Institute (November 2018)

Coulter S, Iosad A, Scales J: *Ending the Big Squeeze on Skills: How to Futureproof Education in England*: Tony Blair Institute for Global Change (IGC) (2022)

China's Ten Regulations for Primary Pupils Quoted in Gever R. (2019)

Dept for Education: Realising the Potential of Technology in Education: A Strategy for Education Providers and the Technology Industry (2019)

Dept for Education: Education Technology (EdTech): Survey 2020-21 by Cooper Gibson Research (2021)

Dept for Education: Implementing School System Reform in 22/23 (May 2022)

Dept for Education: Future Opportunities for Education Technology in England: Vicentini L et al (June 2022)

Dept for Education: Research Report DFE-RR215: Evaluation of the City Challenge Programme: Merryn Hutchings et al: 2010)

Donaldson G: Successful Futures: Independent Review of Curriculum and Assessment Arrangements in Wales (February 2015)

Duxbury V et al: International Baccalaureate Students Studying at UK Higher Education Institutions. How do They Perform in Comparison with A-Level Students? IB Research Dept (April 2021)

Edge Foundation/UCL: Inspection Across the UK: How the Four Nations Intend to Contribute to School Improvement: Munoz-Chereau B & Ehren M (March 2021)

Education Endowment Foundation: Research Schools Programme in Opportunity Areas: Investigating the Impact of Research Schools in Promoting Better Outcomes: Quing Gu et al (October 2021)

Education Policy Institute: A Comparison of School Institutions and Policies Across the UK (April 2023)

Enenkel Kathrin: What can German Reunification Teach the UK about Levelling Up? Centre for Cities (October 14, 2021)

EDSK: A Step Baccward: Analysing the impact of the 'English Baccalaureate' Performance Measure: Richmond Tom (2019)

EDSK: Requires Improvement: A New Role for Ofsted and School Inspections: Richmond Tom (April 2019)

EDSK Free to choose: How 'Individual Educational Budgets' can Revolutionise Tertiary Education: Tom Richmond (May 2019)

EDSK: Trust Issues (September 2019)

EDSK: Post-Qualification Admissions (June 2020)

EDSK: Further Consideration (September 2020)

EDSK: Re-Assessing the Future (Part I & II) (January & April 2021)

EDSK: Making Progress: The Future of Assessment and Accountability in Primary Schools: Richmond T & Regen E (November 2021)

EDSK: Examining Exams (2023)

Fawcett J & Gunson: *Shaping the Future. A 21st Century Skills System for Wales: Challenges and Opportunities*: IPPR (2019)

FEA: Celebrating the Power of Colleges in the Path Forward (August 2023)

FEA: Opportunity England Report (2023)

Freedman Sam: *The exam question: Changing the model of assessment reform*: Institute for Government (August 2022)

Gatley Jane: Can the New Welsh Curriculum achieve its purposes?: The Curriculum Jnl (January 31, 2020)

Gerver Richard: Education: A Manifesto for Change: Bloomsbury Education (2019)

Global Education Evidence Advisory Panel (GEEAP: 2023 Cost-effective Approaches to Improve Global Learning (May 2023)

Global Market Insights (GMI): Industry trends (2020)

Gov. Wales: Education in Wales: Our National Mission: 2017–21 Action Plan

Gov. Wales: Curriculum for Wales: Supporting Learner Progression Assessment Guidance (January 2020/June 2022)

Green Francis & Kynaston: Engines of Privilege: Britain's Private School Problem: Bloomsbury (2019)

Holon IQ: 2023 Global Education Outlook (January 2023)

Hopenbeck T N et al: Evaluation of IB Career-related Programme Implementation in the county of Kent, UK (December 2021).

House of Commons Committee: The Future of post-16 Qualifications: Third Report of Session 2022-23 (April 28, 2023)

House of Lords Liaison Committee Report: AI in the UK: No Room for Complacency (December 2020)

HM Govt: National AI Strategy (2021)

Institute for Fiscal Studies (IFS): Annual Report on Education Spending in England (2022)

Institute for Government: Devolved Public Services: Atkins G, Dalton G. (April 20, 2021)

JISC: Artificial Intelligence (AI) in Tertiary Education (April 2021; updated September 2023)

Johnson Paul: Follow the Money: How Much Does Britain Cost?: Abacus (2023)

Jones Calvin: Fit for the Future: Education in Wales: draft White Paper (October 2019)

JRF/Institute for Government Report: Implementing the London Challenge: Kidson M & Norris E (2014)

Kukulska-Hulme Agnes et al: Innovating Pedagogy: Open University Institute of Educational Technology Innovation Report 10 (2022)

Learning Policy Institute (LPI): Reinventing School in the COVID Era and Beyond: Darling-Hammond L et al (September 2020)

Lough Catherine: *Revealed: Global Best and Worst at 21st-century Skills*: TES Magazine (January 14, 2020)

Ministry of Defence: Global Strategic Trends: The Future Starts Today: Sixth Edition (October 2018)

Muir K: Putting Learners at the Centre: Towards a Future Vision for Scottish Education (March 2022)

National Baccalaureate Trust (NBT): Proposals for a National Baccalaureate for England (March 2022).

National Citizen Service (NCS) programme as a Personal and Social Development Programme for 15–17 year-olds

OECD: Scotland's Curriculum for Excellence: Into the Future (June 2021)

OECD follow-up report (OECD Report on CfE: Implications for Career Services (October 2021)

OECD: Improving Schools in Wales: An OECD Perspective (2014/2015)

OECD: The Welsh Education Reform Journey: A Rapid Policy Assessment (2017)

OECD: Achieving the New Curriculum for Wales (October 2020)

OECD Education Policy Perspectives No 33: Teachers' Professional Learning Study: A Diagnostic Report for Wales; Roy S et al (2021)

OECD: Trustworthy AI in Education: Promises and Challenges (February 2020)

Parry David: The Challenges Facing English Schools in the Journey to 2030, with a Specific Focus on London: London Review of Education: 17 (2): 178–192 (2019)

Paterson Lindsay: Scotland's Curriculum for Excellence: The Betrayal of a Whole Generation? (January 2018)

Pearson School Report: Schools Today, Schools Tomorrow (June 2022)

PWC Strategy: The Future of Government: Levelling up the UK (2021)

Robinson Ken & Aronica Lou: Creative Schools: Penguin (2016)

Seldon Anthony & Abidoye Oladimeji: *The Fourth Education Revolution: Will Artificial Intelligence Liberate Or Infantilise Humanity?*: University of Buckingham Press (2018)

Selwyn Neil: *Is Technology Good for Education?*: Polity (2016)

Selwyn Neil: *Should Robots Replace Teachers? AI and the Future of Education*: Polity Press (2019)

Shapira Marina et al: *Choice Atttainment and Positive Destinations: Exploring the impact of curriculum policy change on young people*: University of Stirling (2023)

Stobart G: Upper-secondary Education Student Assessment in Scotland: a Comparative Perspective: OECD Education Working Paper No 253 (2021)

Strauss V: 'China's 10 New and Surprising School Reform Rules': Washington Post (October 30, 2013)

Sutton Trust: Social Mobility-Past, Present and Future: Eyles A. et al (June 2022)

Sylvester Rachel (chairwoman of the TEC): *The Skills Children Need for Life Are Obvious-we Just Need to Teach Them*: The Times (May 10, 2022)

Times Education Commission: Bringing out the Best: How to Transform Education and Unleash the Potential of Every Child (June 2022)

Tutoring Trust Report: The Future of Tutoring (July 2023)

UNESCO: Concept Note for the 2023 Global Education Monitoring Report on Technology and Education (2023)

Withers J: *Fit for the Future: Developing a Post-school Learning System to Fuel Economic Transformation: Scottish Government* (June 7, 2023)

Wright Katie: International Baccalaureate Longer-Term Outcome; University of Melbourne (January 2015)

Index

For Product Safety Concerns and Information please contact our EU
representative GPSR@taylorandfrancis.com
Taylor & Francis Verlag GmbH, Kaufingerstraße 24, 80331 München, Germany